New Religious Movements Series
Series Editor: Peter B. Clarke

MY SWEET LORD

The Hare Krishna Movement

MY SWEET LORD

The Hare Krishna Movement

KIM KNOTT

Department of Theology and Religious Studies,
University of Leeds

THE AQUARIAN PRESS
Wellingborough, Northamptonshire

First published 1986

© KIM KNOTT 1986

British Library Cataloguing in Publication Data

Knott, Kim
  My sweet lord: the Hare Krishna movement.
  1. Krishna (Hindu deity) — Cult
  I. Title
  294.5155   BL1220

  ISBN 0-85030-432-6

*The Aquarian Press is part of the
Thorsons Publishing Group*

Printed and bound in Great Britain

vancha kalpatarubhyas ca krpa sindhubhya eva ca
patitanam pavanebhyo vaisnavebhyo namo namah

To the devotees, with love and thanks

Contents

Series Editor's Preface

New religions abound in contemporary Britain. As many as five hundred have been established since 1945. These religions derive from many different cultures and have given rise to much controversy in the media and in every walk of life — politics, medicine, education, the law, and the churches.

The methods of recruitment, aims, purposes, rituals, and practices of a number of these movements have all been hotly debated and observers have been led to ask to what extent, if any, some of these movements may reasonably be regarded as religious and enjoy the benefits, for example, of charitable status. On the other hand, there are those who see them as a clear indication of 'the return of the sacred' to modern society, which it was widely assumed was undergoing an inexorable process of secularization.

One thing is clear to those involved in the field of new religions: it is impossible to generalize about them. While a number do hold similar beliefs and pursue similar goals, new religions come in all shapes and sizes and are often very different from one another. That is why it is important to consider each of these religions separately before attempting to reach any overall conclusions concerning the phenomenon of new religions, and this also explains in large measure the purpose of this series.

In each book an attempt will be made to provide an objective account of a particular movement, its origins, development, beliefs, practices, aims, and appeal, and the response to it of the wider society. Some of the controversial issues surrounding these movements will also be discussed and the authors have been given the freedom to express their own opinion, based on the evidence available to them, on these matters. Technical language has been avoided wherever possible with the intention of making the series available to the widest possible readership.

PETER B. CLARKE
King's College, London

Acknowledgements

Like most studies of contemporary religion and religious groups the research for this book has combined several different scholarly methods and approaches. As a result of this it is essential for me to thank a number of people for their help, patience and guidance.

First of all I would like to mention A. C. Bhaktivedanta Swami Prabhupada, the founder of the Hare Krishna movement who died in 1977. Without his efforts not only would there have been no movement to research but the task of understanding and describing the philosophy and practices of Krishna Consciousness would have been virtually impossible. His literary contribution to Hinduism in the West, and his inspiration to others to continue this tradition, must surely be unsurpassed. I would also like to thank His Divine Grace Bhagavandas Goswami Maharaj for the consistent interest he has shown in the progress of this book and for his tolerance, kindness, and advice. In addition, thanks are due to Dhrstadyumna Maharaj and Sivarama Maharaj for putting up with a researcher on the premises with all her clumsiness, inquisitiveness, and slowness to learn.

I have dedicated the book to all Krishna devotees but some in particular deserve a special mention. A number of them spent long hours with me telling me their personal histories, their opinions, their part in the organization of the movement. Without this I could not have constructed the following account. First of all there are Chaitanyacharana dasi and Gaurasundara dasa and their children. Fortunately for me they made the move from Newcastle to Watford at the time I was undertaking the fieldwork for the book. For all the meals and the hospitality, but most of all for the friendship, thank you. Then, for answering my many questions with both informative answers and considerable patience, and for his judicious comments on the manuscript I would like to thank Amita dasa.

I must also mention the president of Bhaktivedanta Manor and his wife, Akhandadhi dasa and Ratnavati dasi. Akhandadhi provided a great deal of useful material for the fourth chapter and inspired me with his cheerful optimism, and Ratnavati looked after me and saw to my needs on many occasions during the fieldwork period. Other devotees who assisted me with their invaluable knowledge and expertise were Namapriya dasi, Vicitravirya dasa, Hari Krishna dasa, Bhajahari dasa, and Rohininandana dasa.

In addition to these, many other members of the movement gave me their time and attention, answered my questions and made me feel at home. Unfortunately they are too many to mention. Thanks anyway, particularly to all devotees at Bhaktivedanta Manor.

Of my friends outside the movement, who inevitably know a lot more about it than they did before, I would particularly like to thank Helen and Tony who read the manuscript and gave me many useful comments.

On a more formal note I would like to acknowledge ISKCON for the use of photographs for this book, and for a variety of other research materials and services. Finally I would like to thank the staff of the Department of Theology and Religious Studies at the University of Leeds for their interest and encouragement, and the series editor, Peter Clarke of King's College, London, for his patience, and for asking me to write this in the first place.

Introduction

It is often said in the Hare Krishna movement that on the path to self-realization one should combine the qualities of vigilance and intelligence. These are also the qualities which might be recommended to someone coming into contact with a group like Hare Krishna for the first time. Unfortunately, however, there has been a general tendency in the past for the public to err on the side of vigilance. Many people have come to the rather hasty conclusion that the Hare Krishna movement is something to be feared, an organization you would not want your son or daughter to get involved with, a group led by wealthy and ruthless individuals with no compassion or sensitivity, and with plans to break up happy family life and to impose intolerable rules on innocent young people.

It is not altogether surprising that the British public has taken this attitude. After all, it is the attitude portrayed on television and in the newspapers of this religious group and of others like it. The 'cults', as they are commonly called, are almost always presented to us as an inseparable corpus of deviant youth movements. They are all portrayed as wedded to anti-social and corrupt practices such as brainwashing and the break-up of families. It is rarely if ever pointed out that these 'cults' include independent groups such as the Hare Krishna movement, the Unification Church, and Subud that are as disparate as the traditions of Hinduism, Christianity, and Islam in which they have their roots. It is rarely if ever recognized that the people who join these groups do so not against their will but in freedom of choice. In addition, it is rarely — if ever — remembered that families are divided, and always have been, not just by their members joining the ranks of the religious but by daughters marrying against the will of their parents, sons bringing disappointment by rejecting their education for a job or their job for an education, and by parents themselves whose married lives so frequently end in divorce and separation.

Most of our knowledge about the Hare Krishna movement and other contemporary religious groups is derived from the media. But is what television, radio, and the newspapers tell us the full story? To be vigilant without being intelligent about a religious group like this can actually do more harm than good. It is now recognized, for example, that the 'deprogramming' techniques used on young people to turn them away from the new religious lives they have chosen are more akin to 'brainwashing' than the practices of the cults which are thus accused.[1] This is a case of the medication being more dangerous than the disease it was intended to cure.

The trouble is, from the media account of these groups, we are not really able to judge whether their members are in need of treatment at all. In fact, if we take this medical analogy seriously for a moment, we find that recent research has shown that people who belong to new religious movements often experience better psychological health than the rest of us.[2] Perhaps the opposite is true then? Perhaps the Hare Krishna devotees are actually less in need of a cure than the rest of us.

If this is the case, that there are benefits to be gained from the way of life of the Hare Krishna devotees, it is certainly impossible to deduce this from the little that is commonly known about them. Almost nothing is known about the way of life of this group or its philosophy, despite the fact that it has been established in this country since 1969, has a committed following of about 9,000, and has close ties with the 300,000 strong Indian Hindu community, the members of which attend many of its religious functions.[3] In addition, what is known about the movement is misleading in two important respects. The first is that the Hare Krishna movement, despite its novelty to us, is not a new religion; the second is that the view we have of young people chanting and dancing in Central London, although not incorrect, is incomplete. Indeed the Hare Krishna devotees continue to catch our eye whilst we are shopping in Oxford Street, but their brothers and sisters are busy serving Krishna in other places and in other ways. It is as though the understanding we have is based solely on a photograph someone took way back in 1969 or 1970.

But if the Hare Krishna movement is not an entirely new phenomenon, neither is it a static one. These two points can be illustrated simultaneously with a brief reference to its history. 'The Hare Krishna movement' is certainly a new name, and what it denotes is certainly new to the West. It was brought to the United States by an Indian *sadhu* named A. C. Bhaktivedanta Swami in 1965.[4] He brought and subsequently taught the philosophy he had learnt from his spiritual master in India. These teachings had been passed down by a succession of spiritual masters from the founder of this particular

A. C. Bhaktivedanta Swami Prabhupada, founder of ISKCON.

form of religious belief and practice, Chaitanya Mahaprabhu. Chaitanya, who lived from 1486-1534, was not responsible for inventing it: we find its philosophy described in the *Bhagavad Gita*, a religious text which was composed long before the birth of Christ. The Hare Krishna movement, more properly known as the International Society for Krishna Consciousness (ISKCON), has its roots in this tradition, the *bhakti* or devotional tradition. The devotees believe and worship as Chaitanya and his followers did in the sixteenth century, and contemporary Indian exponents of this form of religion recognize them as authentic disciples in the Chaitanya tradition.

What this shows us is that the religion practised by the young people we see in Oxford Street is at least as old as Anglicanism. What is more, in the same sense in which Anglicanism has deeper roots, so has Krishna Consciousness. The difference is that Britain is not the native home of this form of religion, while it is clearly the home of Anglicanism. Like any other missionary movement, however, Krishna Consciousness represents a philosophy and a form of religious practice which has been revitalized in a new social and geographical location. In this sense, at least, it has similarities with missionary Christianity in India and Latin America, and with missionary Islam in India and China. In the case of Hare Krishna and the other Eastern religious groups, however, a desire to preach is not tempered with the politics of the sword or colonialism. Theirs is a peaceful religious message, with no other motive than the spiritual enhancement of the lives of those who choose to join them. They are inspired not by a desire to conquer lands and peoples but by Chaitanya's desire to see the path of devotion broadcast 'in every town and village'.[5]

The philosophy and religious practices of the devotees of the movement have remained very close to the teachings popularized in Bengal in the fifteenth and sixteenth centuries. Nevertheless the context in which this core of Krishna devotionalism has been suspended has changed with the passage of time. Even within his own lifetime Chaitanya had to find ways to make his message appealing to those in South India as well as those in the North-East. Today his teachings are available in many languages, in many countries, by word of mouth and through the medium of the printed word. The contexts are many and various: small groups of careful Krishna conscious citizens discuss philosophy in countries in the Communist bloc; whole families of Italians visit their local temples; Japanese women don saris; Indians in Mauritius, the UK, Fiji, Kenya, South Africa, and the Indian sub-continent chant 'Hare Krishna'. Even within Britain itself the practice of Krishna Consciousness is observed not only on the London streets and in Krishna temples but also in the homes of quite ordinary people: factory workers, teachers, taxi drivers, nurses, shopkeepers. Most of those who used to form the movement's 'hippy' membership in the 1960s are now well into their thirties and early forties with homes and children of their own. They still adhere to the same philosophy, the same principles and the same basic lifestyle, but their social position has changed. They have matured, their skills and talents have developed, and their approach to their mission has changed accordingly. In addition, many new, young devotees have joined the movement, along with a growing number of more senior citizens.

The aim of this study is to bridge the divide between the Hare Krishna movement and those outside it. As onlookers, observers and passers-by we are given very little opportunity to understand this colourful but alien phenomenon. I have tried in this account to present the movement and its philosophy largely from the point of view of those involved in it. The material presented in these chapters was gathered from the movement's literature, from interviews with its members, and from an observation of their way of life. The first chapter is historical, describing the development of Krishna Consciousness, its early years in the States and its subsequent rise in this country. The second chapter is sociological, exploring the question of who joins and what kind of commitment they make. Chapter Three provides an account of the beliefs and practices of the Hare Krishna devotees. Chapter Four moves from the participant's perspective to the world outside. In recent years a range of people and institutions have commented upon the Hare Krishna movement, its members and their lifestyle. These include the parents and friends of devotees, the press, the police, Members of Parliament, anti-cult organizations, the Churches, educationalists and scholars of religion. This chapter will look briefly at some of the interchanges between these institutions and the movement itself. Drawing these perspectives together the conclusion then examines this religious movement in context.

Hare Krishna exists in our society as one of a number of religious options open to people. What is interesting is why it exists and continues to attract people, and how it relates to the other religious and social opportunities available at the present time. Only when we have answered these questions can we really know what we are dealing with and what our attitudes and feelings should be.

1

Hinduism and the West: The Rise of Krishna Consciousness

A Familiar Sight   Most people have heard or read about them in the papers or seen them on television. Others have encountered them in far-flung towns and cities: in Glasgow, Worcester, Bristol, at New York's Kennedy Airport, in Amsterdam, in the streets of Bombay. Even in Bombay, where today a Western style of dress and a Western approach to life is apparent, they are a striking and unusual sight. In London's Oxford Street their presence invokes a contrast which momentarily makes us smile and take notice. There we go, with our heads down, shoppers, tourists, workers, private, insular and speechless, amid the traffic noise and the city pollution. There is only the rhythm of footsteps and cars, and the excitement of shop fronts and burger bars. But then there is something else, a movement in the crowd a little further on, the strains of a melody, a flash of orange. Suddenly people have their cameras at the ready. Some have stopped in groups to look and point; others walk on, self-conscious but determined. Here they are, the Oxford Street chanting party, the men in orange robes, their heads shaved but for a topknot or ponytail of hair, the women in bright saris, in blue, green, pink, white or yellow. Smiling, chanting and swaying, they move through the crowd. Some are playing instruments, perhaps finger cymbals or small drums. Some are handing out leaflets about their nearby vegetarian restaurant and temple. They are both familiar and at odds. We all know who they are — it is in the words they are singing — they are the 'Hare Krishnas'. We all know what to expect when we see them because they have been doing this for years now. Nevertheless, they are different. Being accustomed to their appearance and behaviour does not change the fact that we look normal and they do not. Neither does it remove that slight anxiety we feel when they pass by close to us. It is a little like sitting in the front row at the circus or walking past a drunk. It is a possible cause for embarrassment. Will I be the one to be picked on? Will they stop me and talk? Will I appear

Hare Krishna festival, London, early 1970s.

foolish? When it becomes clear that this will not happen we are at leisure to think well of them: they seem happy; they brighten the place up; they're not doing anyone any harm. It is still 'them' and 'us' though.

What is it that explains this division between us? They look and behave differently from us, but why? What do the robes and the ponytails signify? What does the chanting mean? Are they Hindus or Buddhists?

One explanation of the devotees' appearance is the need to be distinctive, to be recognized, to 'stand up and be counted'.[1] Before you can interest people in your wares you must let them know that you are there. That is how it is for the Hare Krishnas. Their unusual self-presentation cannot be ignored. Neither can this style of dress easily be confused with the dress of other spiritual groups. While saffron is a colour often worn by other Eastern religions, the shaved head and the tail of hair remain to distinguish the chanting party from the 'orange' followers of Bhagwan Rajneesh and the Buddhists. Their style of dress, like their beliefs and practices, has its roots in the sub-continent of India. The unusual garments worn by the men are called *dhotis*. Those who are married wear white; those who are celibate wear saffron.[2] Most of them have shaved heads, although some of those whose work keeps them in regular contact with the rest of us keep their hair short. Like their shaven brothers, however, they retain a tail of hair to distinguish them from those outside the Hare Krishna movement. The ponytail or topknot is called a *sikha*. The devotees say it serves to identify them to others as Hare Krishnas, and therefore to remind people of Lord Krishna Himself.[3] The same is true of the marks we see on the noses and foreheads of the chanters. These *tilaka* marks are made from clay, and are generally associated by Indians with the worship of Krishna.[4] The *sari* and the *dhoti* of the Hare Krishna people are said to encourage the devotional sense; in addition, they are loose and comfortable; finally, and perhaps most significantly, they link the devotees in the Hare Krishna movement — in Britain, the USA, Africa, Australasia, or Asia — with a cultural and religious tradition of great antiquity and spirituality. In the Indian context they seem quite normal. The female devotees in their saris look like Indian women in general; the male devotees are easily identifiable as religious men, as *sadhus, sannyasis,* or *swamis.*[5]

Having been struck by their appearance, the next question usually concerns their purpose. What are they singing about, and why do they choose to sing and dance in the streets?

In fact, the words they sing are very simple:

Devotees at Heathrow Airport.

> Hare Krishna, Hare Krishna,
> Krishna Krishna, Hare Hare,
> Hara Rama, Hare Rama,
> Rama Rama, Hare Hare.

Together they form the *maha mantra*, the verse which is of central importance to the devotees and the beliefs they hold. This mantra has been sung all over the world, and will be remembered by many as a top twenty hit from the late 1960s. It is impossible to translate the words of the verse because they are names. The *maha mantra* contains the names of God, and *kirtana* is the congregational chanting of the names of God: 'the word Hara (Hare) is the form of addressing the energy of the Lord, and the words Krishna and Rama are forms of addressing the Lord Himself' [ISKCON, 1982, p. xiii].

Krishna is the central name spoken in the mantra. In the traditional terminology of the Hindu religion Krishna is an *avatara* or incarnation of the God Vishnu. Vishnu is considered to be 'the preserver' in the divine cosmological system. In this role He is thought to have descended and taken human or even animal form at different times when the world was in need of help. [6] Krishna and Rama were both incarnations of Vishnu in this traditional system. The story of Rama is found in the *Ramayana,* the most popular of the Indian epics. He is depicted as a young warrior, with bow and arrows, supported by his wife, Sita, and brother, Lakshman. Together with them and their loyal friend, the monkey Hanuman, Rama overthrew the demon Ravana and returned victorious to rule his land. The story of Krishna is more complex. He appears first in the *Bhagavad Gita* (which forms a section of the *Mahabharata*) as charioteer and counsellor to the warrior Arjuna at the time of the battle of Kurukshetra. The most complete account of his life, however, is given in the *Bhagavata Purana* (generally known by the Hare Krishna movement as *Srimad Bhagavatam*). Krishna is commonly worshipped as a baby, as an attractive young cowherder, and as a powerful ruler: the *Bhagavata Purana* brings these three stages together narrating episodes from Krishna's childhood, youth, and maturity.

In the Hare Krishna movement it is Krishna who is seen as 'the supreme personality of Godhead'. [7] Vishnu is accepted as an 'all pervasive, fully empowered expansion of Lord Krishna' [Prabhupada, 1970, p. 239], but it is Krishna, not Vishnu, who is the focus of devotion, worship, and service. Indeed it is Krishna who incarnates Himself to help the living entities.

In the late nineteenth and early twentieth centuries, largely as a result of the British relationship with the Indian sub-continent, knowledge of and interest in the Indian religious tradition began to grow in the West. Scholars of religion and linguistics worked on the texts of Hinduism. Travellers visited temples and observed religious practices. In addition a number of people in Britain and America began to take an interest in the newly-established Theosophical Society and in the teachings of visiting religious leaders from India. Although the ideas and practices introduced at this time remained of interest to only a small number of people, certain of them took root. Hatha yoga, vegetarianism, the philosophical idea of complete and absolute spiritual Oneness, meditation, reincarnation, and karma became well-established intellectual issues during the mid-twentieth century, and were subsequently revitalized in the 1960s and 1970s by a variety of youth movements. [8] This steady if somewhat esoteric interest in aspects of Indian religion and philosophy tended to stress ideas and practices that were radically different from those available in the culture of Britain and America. They challenged people's attitudes to the health of the body and the mind. They questioned the accepted theological and evolutionary views of life and death, and they introduced a monistic philosophy in which God and the soul or spirit were seen to be indivisible, in which there was an absolute, impersonal Oneness of which we were all seen to be part. [9]

The Theosophical Society, Transcendental Meditation, the Divine Light Mission, and the followers of Bhagwan Rajneesh all subscribe to this monistic religious perspective despite the apparent differences in their practical orientation. But the Hare Krishna movement is an Indian group with a very different philosophical stance. It is a theistic movement. Krishna is a personal God, and the souls are His children. They are, in an important sense, separate from Krishna, and can thus serve and worship Him. Krishna is seen as 'the eternal, all-knowing, omnipresent, all-powerful, and all-attractive personality of Godhead' [ISKCON, n.d., p. 11]. In being all-attractive He is seen and worshipped in a number of different ways by different kinds of people. He can be seen as a master, a child, a lover, a friend, or the supreme unknown.

Krishna is not only worshipped by the devotees of the Hare Krishna movement: He is one of the most popular gods of the Hindu pantheon. Millions of Indians either see Krishna as the supreme deity or worship Him alongside other gods and goddesses such as Shiva, Rama, and Durga. [10] In this country the majority of the Hindu temples established by the Indian community — of which there are about 100 — are dedicated to the worship of Lord Krishna.

In addition to the centrality of Krishna for the Hare Krishna devotees and for many Hindus in India and abroad there is the question of universal monotheism. The founder of the Hare Krishna movement in the West, A. C. Bhaktivedanta Swami Prabhupada, commented frequently on this subject in his writings:

> The major religions of the world — Christian, Hindu, Buddhist and Moslem — believe in some supreme authority or personality coming down from the kingdom of God. In the Christian religion, Jesus Christ claimed to be the son of God and to be coming from the kingdom of God to reclaim conditioned souls. As followers of *Bhagavad Gita* we admit this claim to be true. So basically there is no difference of opinion. In details there may be differences due to differences in culture, climate and people, but the basic principle remains the same — that is, God or His representives come to reclaim conditioned souls. [Prabhupada, 1973, p. 65]

The Hare Krishnas, then, do not see their religion (Krishna Consciousness) or their God (Krishna) as exclusive. They see other monotheistic religions as treading the same path with the guidance of the same supreme being. The differences are essentially those of practice and nomenclature, the most important being the choice of Krishna himself. Their views on this are expressed most clearly in the phrase 'the supreme personality of Godhead'. To worship Krishna is to worship God, but to worship Him in His most attractive form. In this sense worship of Krishna is both easier and more satisfying than the worship of God in other forms. This is the reason for the devotees' choice of Krishna and Krishna Consciousness. Other monotheistic religious systems are not untrue; they are just not as effective.

Therefore, when the devotees chant their famous mantra in Oxford Street they are addressing and remembering Krishna in much the same way as Christians address and remember God in prayer. However, unlike personal prayer, congregational chanting or *kirtana* has a public function. It enables others to hear the names of God in addition to bringing personal benefits to the chanters themselves. Both those who chant and those who listen are given a taste of Krishna.

Chanting in Oxford Street, therefore, has an evangelical quality to it. The hope is that others will find a desire to chant too, albeit in the privacy of their own homes. If they do, the benefits to them are seen to be substantial. For example, chanting 'Hare Krishna' tames 'the wild horses of the mind'; it halts the process of reincarnation; it awakens the chanter's original consciousness [ISKCON, 1982, pp. 81-9]. It also helps to fight anxiety and stress. What is more, it is democratic and universal. Anyone can chant it. It is easy. It has the same effect as chanting other authorized divine names such as 'God' or 'Allah'.

People can hold meetings to glorify the Lord in their respective languages and with melodious songs, and if such performances are executed in an offenceless manner, it is certain that the participants will gradually attain spiritual perfection without having to undergo more rigorous methods . . . all people of the world will accept the holy name of the Lord as the common platform for the universal religion of mankind. [Prabhupada, 1972, *Srimad Bhagavatam*, Canto 1; Part 1, Introduction]

This process — of singing the mantra and dancing together — is considered by the Hare Krishna movement to be the best way for people in the disturbed age in which we now live to serve God, and in effect to save themselves and the world. The exemplary figure they follow is Chaitanya Mahaprabhu.

Chaitanya and the Chaitanya Movement Believed to be an incarnation of Krishna, Chaitanya appeared in sixteenth-century Bengal as a great saint and social reformer. It was Chaitanya who was responsible for popularizing the particular form of devotional activity we see in Oxford Street today. [11] While presenting this simple process of self-realization he was also a learned teacher who had encompassed the works of a number of earlier philosophers. In common with some other leaders and teachers of his time he was a devotee of Krishna. He was part of a tradition of *Vaishnavism,* devotion to Vishnu or Krishna, which had its roots in the *Bhagavad Gita* and in the philosophies of Ramanuja and Madhva. [12] Ramanuja, the earliest of these teachers (twelfth century), had been responsible for providing a philosophical basis for devotionalism. Responding to the earlier non-dualistic interpretation (*advaita vedanta*) by Shankara (ninth century) of a text known as the *Brahma Sutra* or *Vedanta Sutra,* Ramanuja compiled a commentary on the same work emphasizing the relationships between the world, the human body, the soul, and God from a theistic perspective. [13] His approach became known as *visishtadvaita* or qualified non-dualism. Madhva, however, whose work was also theistic in orientation, went still further than Ramanuja in underlining the distinction between the souls and God, thus giving much greater attention to the importance of moral questions. Madhva (thirteenth century) taught a strict form of dualism (*dvaita*), and based much of his work on the *Bhagavata Purana*, the story of Krishna.

There were several other medieval religious leaders who contributed to this philosophical debate. Krishna became a focus for most of these, although not all of them subscribed to the dualistic understanding of God and the soul, or a personal relationship between the two. Nimbarka (thirteenth century) formed a sect which was different again from its philosophical forebears. His interpretation was known as *dvaitadvaita* or dualistic non-dualism. It held that at one and the same time God was both the same as and different from the individual souls.

This brings us to Chaitanya who, like Nimbarka, subscribed to this view of 'identity-in-difference'. Chaitanya left only eight verses himself but he inspired his disciples to contribute to the body of Indian philosophical and devotional literature. Chaitanya's own contribution was more immediate and practical. He was a travelling preacher who is said to have influenced a great many Indians in both the North and South with his beliefs and practices. He did a great deal to encourage the love and worship of Krishna and popularized the practice of *kirtana*, of chanting the names of the Lord to an accompaniment of percussion and dancing.

After Chaitanya's death in 1534 the movement he had initiated began to decline in popularity. He had been a leader renowned for his charisma, and for his fervent and emotional love for Krishna. This was hard to sustain in his absence. What followed was a period of philosophical consolidation. Chaitanya's disciples continued to teach, and began to write down the philosophy and the biographical details of their master. In Bengal the movement was perpetuated by two of Chaitanya's closest followers, Advaitacharya and Nityananda, while in Vrndavana (the childhood home of Krishna) six *goswamis* carried on Chaitanya's work at his request. In addition to stressing the importance of the *Bhagavad Gita* and the *Bhagavata Purana* the early disciples produced a number of important manuals and treatises, in Bengali and Sanskrit. Perhaps the most important of these — at least from the perspective of the Hare Krishna movement — were Sanatana Goswami's *Hari-bhakti-vilasa*, a manual of ritual, the *Bhakti-rasamrta-sindhu*, a theological treatise by Rupa Goswami (translated into English by Prabhupada and entitled *The Nectar of Devotion*, considered to be the law book of the Krishna Consciousness movement), and Krsnadasa Kaviraja's *Caitanya-caritamrta*, a biography. These early devotees passed their teachings on to their own followers, who later did the same, and in this way the philosophy and practice attributed to Chaitanya has come down to the present day. Despite inevitable disagreements and rifts between different branches of the tradition this spiritual lineage has succeeded in preserving the essentials of this form of devotionalism, not least of all the practice of *kirtana*. [14]

Abhay Charan De (Prabhupada)   After the first generation of disciples there was a poetic flourishing of the Chaitanya movement in the seventeenth century, largely inspired by the work of three men,

Srinivasa Acharya, Narottama Dasa, and Syamasundara Dasa. This renewal was not sustained, however, and it was not until the end of the nineteenth century that the movement was again revitalized. In 1886 a prominent magistrate and *Vaishnava* scholar named Bhaktivinoda Thakura established the *Gaudiya Vaishnava Mission* with the intention of propagating the beliefs and practices of Chaitanya Mahaprabhu. The mission claimed descent from one of Chaitanya's six *goswamis*, Jiva Goswami, and was continued after Bhaktivinoda Thakura's death by his son Bhaktisiddhanta Sarasvati Goswami. It was this man who in 1933 initiated the founder of the Hare Krishna movement, Prabhupada, or Abhay Charan De as he was formerly known.

Abhay Charan De (1896-1977) had first met his spiritual master, Bhaktisiddhanta Sarasvati, in 1922. At that time and until his retirement in the 1950s he worked in the pharmaceutical industry, first as a manager in a chemical laboratory, then as a pharmaceutical salesman in Allahabad. Throughout this period he was a householder with a wife and children to support. [15]

Despite his domestic responsibilities Abhay remained true to the Gaudiya Vaishnava Mission and to the principles of Krishna devotionalism (*bhakti*) it espoused. But constantly he felt he should be doing more to serve Krishna and his brothers in the Mission. Bhaktisiddhanta Saraswati had stressed the importance of writing and publishing in a conversation with Abhay in 1935, and then, two weeks before his death in 1936, the spiritual master followed this message with another:

> I am fully confident that you [Prabhupada] can explain in English our thoughts and arguments to the people who are not conversant with the languages [Bengali and Hindi] . . . This will do much good to yourself as well as your audience. I have every hope that you can turn yourself into a very good English preacher. [Goswami, 1983 (a), p. xxi]

Abhay now felt he had an idea of how best he could serve his spiritual master. In his earliest conversation with him in 1922, Bhaktisiddhanta had mentioned the need to spread Chaitanya's message worldwide by writing and publishing books. His later statements seemed to confirm this ideal, of preaching and publishing outside the subcontinent of India to those with no knowledge of the beliefs and practices of Chaitanya.

Abhay's first step towards achieving this was to begin writing, publishing, and distributing a magazine called *Back to Godhead*. Throughout the 1940s he worked to produce regular issues of the magazine and began to compile a commentary on the *Bhagavad Gita*.

This was all done in the context of his family life. Then, in the early 1950s, he made the decision to leave his wife and home and to devote the remainder of his life to preaching and writing Chaitanya's message of Krishna consciousness. He was nearly sixty by this time, and in keeping with Indian religious customs decided that he had fulfilled his responsibilities and was now ready to withdraw from material commitment and attachment. In 1959 he took formal renunciation (*sannyasa*) and became a *sannyasi* in order to dedicate himself fully to the task of preaching. It was then that he was given the name Abhay Caranavinda Bhaktivedanta Swami.

Bhaktivedanta Swami (who later became known affectionately as 'Prabhupada') spent the next five years working on his publications. Like those who had come before him in the line of spiritual succession he decided to prepare a commentary on the *Bhagavata Purana*. His work, *Srimad Bhagavatam,* was not to be in Bengali but in English. Although he could get no publisher to agree to publish the many volumes he expected the work to stretch to, he did obtain financial help with publishing the first three volumes privately. Then, in 1965, with no family ties and responsibilities, Prabhupada decided the time had come to leave India to begin his preaching mission abroad. To this end he was given help and support by several far-sighted acquaintances. One man obtained a sponsor for him in the United States, and a businesswoman gave him a place on one of her steamships [Goswami, 1983(b), p. xxxvii]. In August 1965 Prabhupada, together with several trunkloads of his books, set sail from Calcutta bound for the United States.

On 19 September the steamship sailed into New York. Prabhupada was alone, and he was different.

> He was dressed appropriately for a resident of Vrndavana. He wore kanthi-mala (neck beads) and a simple cotton dhoti, and he carried japa-mala (chanting beads) and an old cadar or shawl. His complexion was golden, his head shaven except for the sikha in the back, his forehead decorated with the whitish Vaishnava tilaka. He wore pointed white rubber slippers, not uncommon for sadhus in India. But who in New York had ever seen or dreamed of anyone appearing like this Vaishnava? He was possibly the first Vaishnava sannyasi to arrive in New York with uncompromised appearance. Of course, New Yorkers have an expertise in not giving much attention to any kind of strange new arrival. [Goswami, 1983(b), p. 5)]

Prabhupada's first year in the United States was a continuous expression of this tension. Throughout that period he found himself in places and situations, with old people and young people, Indians and Americans, where and for whom he must have seemed unusual,

Prabhupada with friends and colleagues.

even a little eccentric. Eyebrows were rarely raised, however, and the Swami was always welcomed and never greeted with shock or outrage. Despite this tolerant response it was not until Prabhupada had moved away from the middle-class American circles to which he was first introduced that he began to make real progress with his preaching. He moved unwittingly to a poor district of New York City, to a studio on the Bowery. Here, through various friends he had made, he began to be visited by growing numbers of young people: artists, musicians, students, some of whom had been to India and had an interest in Indian religion and philosophy, many of whom were experimenting in a range of novel pastimes and experiences from macrobiotic cooking and meditation to drug taking. These young people in many ways understood Prabhupada better than the other Indians and Americans he had met since his arrival. They were all seeking something, an experience or a way of life, peace or ecstasy, individual realization or communal security. Many of them did not know what they were looking for but were happy to listen to Prabhupada just as they were happy to try Zen or Yoga. To them he was familiar in the sense that he looked like the *sadhus* and *swamis* some had met in India or others had seen in pictures in books about Indian religion. He talked with them about the *Bhagavad Gita,* which some of them had heard of. He made them chant *mantras.* He cooked and ate vegetarian food. He played Indian music. Because of the cultural and religious appeal Prabhupada had for these young people they continued to visit him, to talk to him, to attend his meetings, and take his advice on spiritual matters. [16]

In June 1966 Prabhupada moved from the Bowery to Second Avenue in the Lower East Side. There, in what had been a shop (with the sign 'Matchless Gifts' from its previous incarnation as a gift shop), he set up a temple and quarters in which he could write and sleep. The following month Prabhupada set up the International Society for Krishna Consciousness (ISKCON). In the charter which he drew up he outlined the main purposes of the society as the propagation of spiritual knowledge and a consciousness of Krishna as revealed in the *Bhagavad Gita* and the *Srimad Bhagavatam,* the teaching of Chaitanya's system of congregational chanting of the names of God, and the publication and distribution of periodicals, magazines and books [Goswami, 1980, pp. 131-3]. The movement for Krishna consciousness was well and truly under way. Prabhupada initiated his first disciples on 9 September 1966, and performed the marriage ceremony for Mukunda and Janaki, two new initiates, on 12 September. Then, about a week later, he led them in their first public *kirtana.* This event, and the feelings it engendered in the young

Hare Krishna in the USA, late 1970s.

disciples, is described in Prabhupada's biography:

> He [Prabhupada] never made a secret of what he was doing. He used
> to say, 'I want everybody to know what we are doing.' Then one day,
> D-day came. He said, 'We are going to chant in Washington Square
> Park.' Everyone was scared. You don't just go into a park and chant.
> It seemed like a weird thing to do. But he assured us, saying, 'You won't
> be afraid when you start chanting. Krsna will help you.' And so we
> trudged down to Washington Square Park, but we were very upset
> about it. Up until that time, we weren't exposing ourselves. I was upset
> about it, and I know that several other people were, to be making a
> public figure of yourself. [Goswami, 1980(a), p. 193]

But the chanting turned out to be less frightening than they had
anticipated, and with Prabhupada they returned to Second Avenue
'elated and victorious. They had broken the American silence'
[Goswami, 1980(a), p. 185].

Since that first public *kirtana* in 1966, the Hare Krishna devotees
have continued to break the silence in countries throughout the world,
in Britain and other European countries, in South Africa, Uganda and
Kenya, Australia, the Americas, Iran and Israel, South East Asia, and
in India itself. The chanting, dancing, and preaching (*sankirtana*),
first performed by Chaitanya in the sixteenth century, has found its
way onto the London streets. [17]

The History of the Hare Krishna Movement in Britain   Despite the
speed with which Prabhupada established his society and his New
York temple it was not for another two years that the devotees came
to Britain. During the intervening period, however, considerable
progress was made in North America. In the winter of 1966-7 premises
were found by Mukunda and Janaki in San Francisco for conversion
into a temple. Prabhupada visited the West coast in January 1967,
officially opened 'New Jagannatha Puri', as the temple was called, and
attended the 'Mantra Rock Dance' at the Avalon Ballroom in the city.
To introduce Krishna Consciousness to the West coast and to help the
financing of the new temple, this concert brought together some of
the then-famous names in rock music (The Grateful Dead, Moby
Grape, Big Brother and the Holding Company) and Prabhupada in
an evening of music and devotion. Not surprisingly, the Hare Krishnas
got off to a popular start with the young in San Francisco.

In New York the devotees were concentrating on the question of
publishing. In the ISKCON charter the production of books and
periodicals had been stated as one of the main aims of the society.
Prabhupada worked away at his translation of the *Srimad Bhagavatam;*
the devotees, under instruction from their spiritual master, began to

compile and print the *Back to Godhead* magazine, the periodical which Prabhupada had first produced in India during the 1940s.

Plans for the growth and development of the movement were extensive: Prabhupada wanted to return to India with several disciples to take the first steps in establishing ISKCON in his homeland, and a number of devotees wished to take the movement to other American cities and to open temples there. By the summer of 1968 these plans had been realized. Prabhupada had left two disciples working for ISKCON in India, and centres had been established in Boston, Los Angeles, Buffalo, and a number of other North American cities.

By this time Prabhupada was very keen to introduce Krishna Consciousness to Britain. In the 1930s one of his own godbrothers from the Gaudiya Vaishnava Mission had travelled from India to England to preach. Bon Maharaj, as he had been called, had stayed for a short time and had lectured largely to the same elderly, middle-class audiences who also listened to speakers from the Ramakrishna Mission, and the Theosophical Society at that time.[18] Ultimately, he had been unsuccessful in attracting genuine followers, and had returned to India. Prabhupada's early experience in the United States told him that success was not to be found in confining one's preaching to an established middle-class set. He decided not to go to England himself in the first place, but to send his young devotees — as he had to San Francisco, Boston and Los Angeles — to find a centre for activities and begin making contacts.

In August 1968 three married couples, Mukunda and Janaki, Syamasundara and Malati, and Gurudasa and Yamuna, came to London. They settled in a flat in Herne Hill, began a regular evening programme, and started to get themselves more widely known. One of their major campaigns was to establish contact with The Beatles, and to this end they made visits and sent food (*prasadam*, spiritual, vegetarian food) and a tape to Apple Records. They got nowhere to begin with. Those who ran day-to-day affairs at the company's headquarters ignored their requests and gestures. Fortunately, one of the devotees was visiting Apple Records one day in the hope of success when George Harrison arrived and immediately spotted him because of his robes and shaven head. George had known about Prabhupada and the movement for several years but had never met any of the devotees before. For both him and for Syamasundara the meeting was opportune.[19] Syamasundara was invited to lunch with George and the other Beatles the following day. An important and fruitful relationship had been established.

George Harrison with devotees at Apple Studios, 1971. (Camera Press, London).

At about the same time (the winter of 1968-9) the devotees were attempting to find more suitable premises for their work. First of all they were offered temporary warehouse space in the Covent Garden area, in Betterton Street. This was ideal because of its central location. The devotees settled in, began to attract local artists and musicians from an Arts Lab nearby, and invited members of the Indian community to the little temple they had set up. Just as Prabhupada had made the *kirtana* the focus of his early work in New York, so the devotees encouraged all their visitors to chant the Hare Krishna *mantra*. In the late summer of 1969 the devotees moved to Bury Place, near the British Museum. They had already received their first major publicity, in the 'Atticus' column of the *Sunday Times Magazine*. In mid-1969, however, the devotees, with the help of George Harrison, recorded the Hare Krishna Mantra, at Apple studios. It was released as a single in August, a year after their arrival in Britain. On the first day the record sold 70,000 copies. It was so successful that it reached the Top Twenty in England, and the devotees appeared on BBC1's 'Top of the Tops' programme. George Harrison recalls these events in an interview with Mukunda, one of the devotees who took part in recording the mantra:

> I figured this is the space age, with airplanes and everything. If everyone can go around the world on their holidays, there's no reason why a mantra can't go a few miles as well. So the idea was to try to spiritually infiltrate society, so to speak. After I got Apple Records committed to you and the record released, and after our big promotion, we saw it was going to become a hit. And one of the greatest things, one of the greatest thrills of my life, actually, was seeing you all on BBC's 'Top of the Pops'. I couldn't believe it. It's pretty hard to get on that programme, because they only put you on if you come into the Top 20. It was just like a breath of fresh air. My strategy was to keep it to a three-and-a-half-minute version of the mantra so they'd play it on the radio, and it worked . . . It was the greatest fun of all, really, to see Krsna on 'Top of the Pops'. [ISKCON, 1982, pp. 15-16]

The success of the record coincided with Prabhupada's first visit in Britain in September 1969. Because of problems the devotees were experiencing over moving the temple into a house in Bury Place John Lennon had suggested they stay at Tittenhurst — his Berkshire estate — in exchange for helping with some renovation work. So it was John Lennon's white Rolls Royce that carried Prabhupada away after his Heathrow reception, and it was at Tittenhurst that he stayed for his first seven weeks in Britain, discussing plans with his devotees, meeting George Harrison, and John and Yoko, dictating his latest work (*Krsna, the Supreme Personality of Godhead*), and walking in the grounds of the estate [Goswami, 1982, Chapter Two]. In addition, he began a programme of lectures at venues such as Camden Town Hall, Conway Hall in Central London, and Oxford Town Hall. These were attended by a mixed audience of British and Indians, and served to convince Prabhupada and his devotees of the growing need to establish their centre in Bury Place where regular meetings could be held.

During the autumn of 1969 the movement became widely known throughout Europe. The 'Hare Krishna Mantra' reached the Top Ten in a number of European countries, and the devotees were often invited to perform at concerts with professional groups. Prabhupada appeared on the popular chat show, 'Late Night Line-Up', and travelled to Amsterdam to appear on Dutch television. The press took an interest in the relationship between the Hare Krishnas and The Beatles: a photograph in the *Daily Sketch* showed Prabhupada and his devotees eating in the grounds at Tittenhurst with the caption 'Krishna people dine out at John and Yoko's place'.

The most important event to occur during Prabhupada's first visit to this country was the opening of the temple in Bury Place. The date was set for the 14 December, and by the time the day had arrived the room had been prepared, the altar had been completed, and statues of Krishna and his consort, Radha, had been donated by a London Hindu society. The BBC filmed the opening ceremony during which Prabhupada officially installed the deities. It was the twenty-first temple he had opened in three years, but it was ISKCON's first foothold in Europe. ISKCON now has centres in at least forty countries. The movement has published books — generally referred to as 'transcendental literature' — in about fifty languages, including Ethiopian, Laotian, Arabic, and Chinese. Millions of people have visited centres the world over. To describe the historical details of the expansion of the movement would require more space than is available here. Several developments have had a particular impact, however, and two of these occurred as early as 1970.

Soon after the opening of the London temple Prabhupada declared his intention to establish a central authority within ISKCON, a 'Governing Body Commission'. The GBC, which was formed in July 1970, was to be composed of a dozen disciples who would act as Prabhupada's representatives. The individual temples and centres were to remain independent and self-financing but the GBC members were to act as zonal secretaries, co-ordinating the affairs of these local bodies, and as executors in the event of Prabhupada's death. At the same time Prabhupada initiated another scheme, the Bhaktivedanta Book Trust (BBT). He made several of his disciples trustees, and stipulated that they should aim to publish and distribute transcendental literature to fund both the establishment of temples throughout the world and the continued publication of books. The Governing Body Commission and the Bhaktivedanta Book Trust have functioned to centralize what

Prabhupada in India.

over the years has become a multi-national concern.

Since the death of Prabhupada in 1977 the GBC and the BBT have shouldered the responsibility for the maintenance and continuity of Krishna Consciousness. The Governing Body Commission has met to decide on international policy, and to monitor the zones under its authority. The Bhaktivedanta Book Trust, centred in Los Angeles but with branches elsewhere, has continued to publish the writings and translations of Prabhupada, and other related works such as the biography of the founder, vegetarian cookery books, a book of devotional song lyrics, etc. In addition to these overarching, organizational structures, before his death Prabhupada gave the instruction that some of his disciples should become gurus, with the responsibility for initiating future devotees into Krishna Consciousness. Prabhupada selected these initiating gurus himself, and made it clear that the people they were to initiate would become their own disciples and his 'granddisciples' [Goswami, 1983(a), pp. 324-5].

It is these three provisions — the GBC, the BBT, and the continuation of the spiritual lineage or succession of gurus — which have ensured not only the maintenance of the movement around the world, but its continuity with the principles and practices laid down by Prabhupada in the tradition of Chaitanya devotionalism. In any particular area the survival of the group depends on the faith and commitment of the devotees to the cause of Krishna Consciousness, but the wider movement (ISKCON) can function only by combining local initiatives with international organization.

The history of the Hare Krishna movement in Britain in recent years provides an example of the way in which these two levels have operated together to push Krishna Consciousness forward.

Before Prabhupada died in 1977 he made his last visit to Bhaktivedanta Manor, the house near Watford which George Harrison had bought for the devotees in 1973. His decision to come to Britain from India, which had by this time become the centre of his activities, despite illness, was largely in recognition of the success of the movement in Britain at that time. The British devotees, by following Prabhupada's instructions and by working enthusiastically and tirelessly, were now leading the world in book distribution. Their preaching campaign was at its peak. The spirit of Krishna Consciousness was reaching large numbers of people by the route identified by Prabhupada's own spiritual master forty years earlier.

It is very hard to imagine how the devotees coped after the death in 1977 of Prabhupada in Vrndavana, India. Each one must have felt both desolated by his absence and motivated to go on in the service of Krishna in his memory. He had told his followers on many occasions that 'Wherever you are is Vrndavana', the village in India where Krishna had spent his childhood years and a place greatly revered by all Vaishnavites. He had said that to be chanting the Hare Krishna mantra was to be in Vrndavana; to be preaching Krishna Consciousness in Britain or the United States or Africa was to be in Vrndavana. And to die in Vrndavana was to be guaranteed of attaining 'eternal Vrndavana'. Therefore, for the devotees to continue wholeheartedly in Prabhupada's service, and ultimately in the service of Krishna, was for them to be close to their spiritual master. They had to serve 'in separation' but this was seen as the highest service of all: the same service that Radha and the other loving devotees of Krishna (the *gopis*) had performed after He had left them to move on to other commitments in Mathura.

Prabhupada's British disciples were practically assisted by the continuity provided by ISKCON in the form of the Governing Body Commission and the initiating guru for this area, Jayatirtha dasa, who took over the responsibility for the organization. Although devotees in this country, like those the world over, were in great distress at this time, old schemes continued to bring good results and new initiatives were introduced. A training programme for new recruits to the movement had already been set up in the mid-1970s, and it continued to have considerable success after Prabhupada's death. The following year the London temple moved from Bury Place to a more central position in Soho Street. The new site contained a restaurant as well as a temple, and became an attraction for many people with an interest in the movement and its philosophy.

As a result of cumulative efforts throughout the 1970s the Hare Krishna movement in Britain began to experience considerable success in 1977 and 1978. A booklet produced at that time stated that some 1,500 visitors attended Bhaktivedanta Manor near Watford each Sunday, and hundreds of other people had come into contact with the movement at the time of its annual processions through the streets of London, Leicester and Birmingham. [20] In addition, the new recruitment methods were working well, and considerable numbers of people were joining the introductory courses offered.

This boom period created a need for more facilities and thus culminated in the acquisition of a large, stately property in Worcestershire in 1979. The purchase of Croome Court, or 'Chaitanya College' as it became known, was necessitated by the general expansion in the state of operations in the movement during this period. Not only was recruitment successfully bringing new members to Krishna Consciousness but more existing members, with the passing of time, were getting married and having children. Clearly the requirements

Bhaktivedanta Manor.

of these families were quite different from the more basic needs of single devotees whose main work was chanting and preaching from door to door or on the streets. More privacy in domestic life was required, and the educational needs of the children had to be met. Chaitanya College provided a more pastoral setting for family life than the London temple, and greater opportunity for expansion than the main headquarters at Bhaktivedanta Manor. In addition, as bureaucratic and business operations were also expanding, this new property provided greater facility for centralizing the British division of the Bhaktivedanta Book Trust, administrative affairs, and, in due course, such ventures as the mail order department, a recording studio, and an educational museum. 'Plenty of Scents', a branch of the Los Angeles ISKCON incense manufacturers, was established nearby.

Croome Court, built in the mid-eighteenth century for the sixth Earl of Coventry, had formerly been a Roman Catholic boys' school. Although it was used to fulfil a number of purposes by the Hare Krishna movement, not least of all as living quarters for some two hundred devotees, its educational use was retained. In February 1980 a school or *gurukula* was opened for children of infant and primary school age. Trained teachers taught the children a full range of ordinary school subjects as well as classes of a religious nature. When government inspectors visited the school to examine the kind of education it offered, they gave it their qualified approval. [21]

In the early 1980s the British mission was geographically divided between Chaitanya College in Worcestershire and Bhaktivedanta Manor in Hertfordshire, with a persistent presence in the old haunts around Oxford Street in Central London. To some degree this spatial division bore a relation to the major initiatives within the movement during these years, to the 'Friends of Lord Krishna' (FOLK) programme which worked with people in their homes, the Indian Community Affairs Programme, and to the continuing *sankirtana* programme of public preaching and chanting. [22]

Achievements in these three areas were disturbed in 1982 by the departure of the guru responsible for Great Britain, Jayatirtha dasa. After seriously contravening the basic regulative principles of Krishna Consciousness and after protracted efforts at rehabilitation he was offered an ultimatum by the Governing Body Commission of ISKCON which encouraged him to leave. [23] The impact of this event was potentially devastating. Many devotees had been initiated by Jayatirtha. Some were working towards initiation. Others, particularly Prabhupada's old disciples in the region, had given him their loyal support and allegiance. It was difficult for Jayatirtha's disciples to know what to think or do in response to this calamity. By taking him as their

spiritual master they had entered into a reciprocal spiritual relationship with him. Could he really have broken this trust? Was he really out of line with the other initiating gurus in ISKCON, with the Governing Body Commission, and, more importantly, the teachings of his own spiritual master, Bhaktivedanta Swami Prabhupada? A large number, particularly of Jayatirtha's personal disciples, left the movement with him, although after a while some returned to the fold.

Not only had the spiritual leader been removed but the Hare Krishna movement in Britain had lost considerable impetus. Even after the new initiating guru had been assigned to Britain it was a long time before calm returned. [24]

The movement has since made gradual progress in regaining its lost stability. The events of 1982 are now seen as a valuable part of the learning process of the path of Krishna Consciousness. [25] Each and every devotee as a consequence of Jayatirtha's 'fall' had to examine their own behaviour, their own future in the movement, and their own relationship to the spiritual and organizational leadership within ISKCON. The current spiritual master, Bhagavandas Goswami Maharaj ('Srila Gurudeva' to the devotees), with the help of a loyal, local leadership, has succeeded in bringing new unity and purpose to the movement in Britain. Chaitanya College has now been sold, the money from the sale being used to settle the financial instability brought on in recent years, to invest for the future, and to publish and reprint books in order to maintain the advancement of Prabhupada's vision of book distribution.

Since 1969 the Hare Krishna movement in Britain has had a varied and interesting history. It started noisily with a hit record and a fruitful relationship with The Beatles. [26] It attracted considerable numbers of young people at a time when the spiritual quest was a popular and respectable path to follow. Since then it has developed a valuable working relationship with the Indian Hindu community, and has made inroads into ordinary social life with its Friends of Lord Krishna (FOLK) programme. It has pursued the rural ideal, and yet also made a name for itself on the streets of Central London. It has suffered near collapse, has managed to grow out of that experience with renewed vitality, and throughout the movement in Britain there now seems to be an optimistic attitude to the future.

2

The Hare Krishna Devotees: Continuity and Change

It is a not uncommonly held view that the members of new religious movements are similar kinds of people before they join up, and mirror images of one another after a few months of the 'brainwashing'. In fact devotees come from a range of social backgrounds. They are of different ages when they join. They have different tastes. Their talents differ. As a result, the tasks the devotees perform within the movement, the skills they acquire, and their attitudes to spirituality and the more practical aspects of life are very different.

It is easy, however, for those outside the movement to observe the brightly clad chanters, and to conclude that their strange behaviour is the result of a common cause. Those who join the Hare Krishna movement, like those in other new religions have been variously portrayed by outsiders as drug addicts, disaffected students, the products of broken homes and unhappy families, and hippies. The more established leadership is equally pigeon-holed: child-snatchers, breakers of families, financial racketeers. It is certainly true that the Hare Krishna movement, like all other groups and institutions, contains its fair share of fanatics, evangelicals, workaholics and deviants; but like any group, it is a microcosm of a society with problems, a society comprised of diverse people with diverse personalities, qualities, opinions, and approaches to life.

These personal differences do not obscure the one thing held in common by the devotees, the basic philosophy of Krishna Consciousness. Neither do they deny the fact that most of those now in the movement were seeking something before they joined. That they all had a general desire to give their lives order and meaning, however, is saying very little of any sociological significance. After all, people get involved in any number of different individual or collective pursuits for the very same reasons. [1]

The Full-time Devotees   Since its early days in New York, Krishna Consciousness has attracted new recruits for very ordinary human reasons, though in the 1960s and early 1970s there was a more pronounced trend amongst young people in particular towards alternative 'ways of being' rather than traditional paths of self-fulfilment. This brief period and the 'happenings' which were a part of it are referred to as the 'counter-culture' because, in general, they represented the desire of the young both to cast aside the roles they were expected to play, and to take up alternatives. [2] Underlying the trappings of these new and alternative lifestyles, however, were important and timeless moral questions. What is the best way to spend an all-too-brief life-span of seventy or eighty years? Do marriage and traditional family life provide happiness for couples and their children? Is this really a sensible way to live, at war, surrounded by consumer durables, a victim of capitalism? Why can't we be nicer to each other? Where is God in all of this?

It is against this general cultural background that the early history of the Hare Krishna movement in the West is best viewed. In the late 1960s in America many young people were not only socially and philosophically disaffected, but they had new toys at their fingertips. Aspects of religion and culture from the East, as well as drugs, were part of the novelty. They were passionately adopted, tried, and very often hastily rejected by the young, particularly by those who were middle-class and well-educated. Everyone was seeking, and Hare Krishna was just one of the myriad of possible curiosities to try on the search. It had some of the popular features such as a vital link with the East, strange clothes and unusual practices, vegetarian food and a form of meditation. However, in other respects it was, in counter-cultural terms, unorthodox. The basic principles of the movement militated against what had become new and accepted norms. They frowned upon drug-taking and sexual freedom. Discipline and austerity were valued, not 'loose living'. In addition, the view of gender roles internalized by the devotees did not appeal to those in American society who supported the cause of liberation for women. As a result of these factors its major appeal must have been to those who had participated fully in the counter-cultural search but who had not found what they were looking for. In this sense, it was 'counter counter-cultural' [Daner, 1976, p. 104].

Despite this, the Hare Krishna movement sought to fulfil basic human needs. It provided new members with a sense of purpose ('Krishna Consciousness'), with a sense of community, with the opportunity to break unwanted habits, with friends, with food, with love. It also offered personal spiritual guidance in the form of the guru and founder, Prabhupada.

This combination, of the fulfilment of basic needs in an exotic cultural setting, drew many young people to the movement in the late 1960s, first in New York, then on the West Coast of the United States, and then, in 1969, in Britain. Of the twenty-five initiated in Britain at the beginning, about fifteen remain. Most of these have moved abroad to extend the missionary base, but a number of Prabhupada's early disciples have made the UK their home. The current guru for this zone, Bhagavandas Goswami Maharaj, is an American, and the two *sannyasis* resident here, Dhrstadyumna Swami and Sivarama Swami, are American and Canadian respectively. Many of the other leading devotees are Americans or are 'Prabhupada disciples' from other countries. In addition, important positions are occupied by early disciples born in the UK.

It has always been extremely difficult to quantify the full-time membership of the movement either nationally or internationally. Complex records are now kept, but this was not always the case. Occasionally people leave a temple, but they may well continue to practise the principles of Krishna Consciousness outside. In what sense are they to be counted? Then there are those British devotees working in temples around the world. How are they to be taken into consideration? The task of estimating the size of the movement is a difficult one. The results of such an exercise are also fairly misleading. Before the sale of Chaitanya College in 1984 it was said that there were approximately 300 full-time devotees in Britain, but this tells us very little about the state of the movement here and now or its likely future. [3]

More revealing about the contemporary state of the movement are recent initiations. At the British ceremony in 1984 young Indians, West Indians, and Africans were initiated along with young Anglo-Saxons. In addition, a number of older people took part. One man in his eighties had been specially recommended for initiation, and a senior Indian gentleman was also accepted. The new disciples had come from very different occupations and family situations. Some were young and unemployed. Some were married: in several cases both husband and wife were initiated. One woman was head of a department in a large American company. One of the men had given up a £50,000-a-year job with a well-known property development company in order to work for the movement.

Though it would be very hard to generalize about the social composition of this particular group of initiates, the common factor is that they *wanted* to be initiated. [4] All of them had been developing a commitment to the philosophy and lifestyle of Krishna Consciousness for at least a year, some for considerably longer. Most had attended the three-month introductory programme. They had come to this because of an attraction to the beliefs and practices of the movement kindled by reading one of Prabhupada's books, meeting devotees, or experiencing the food and the rituals, and so on.

In some senses this attraction is similar to the initial adherence motives of the counter-cultural devotee; but although past and present initiates shared what is commonly called a 'taste' for Krishna Consciousness, they differ in many other respects. Those in positions of authority within the British division of ISKCON distinguish between the formative years of the movement, when initiation was given lightly in order both to encourage devotees and to increase the preaching potential, and recent years, when new people have had to demonstrate the seriousness of their intentions and their maturity before initiation is granted. Nowadays, quality rather than quantity is the operative principle in deciding who is to be initiated. The opportunities for practising Krishna Consciousness without joining an austere community of devotees are now considerably greater than they were in the early 1970s, with the results that only exceptional candidates with a true vocation for the life are accepted for initiation, and fewer leave the movement.

Since 1976 statistics have been kept on numbers entering the introductory training programmes and receiving initiation. In total over 350 people have received initiation since that time. It is almost certain that nearly double that figure took part in the training but that around half did not pursue initiation because they were unready to commit themselves to the way of life or the philosophy. Of the 350 full-timers who joined between 1976 and 1983 the majority have remained in the movement. [5] Most reside in the UK (41 per cent) but 15 per cent work abroad, giving a total of 56 per cent still full-time in ISKCON. Of the remainder, the movement has lost contact with 14 per cent, and 5 per cent have left full-time service (although most of these retain the principles on an informal basis). However, 25 per cent of those initiated during this period left directly as a result of the leadership problems in 1982. In fact, the figure (of 89 devotees) was higher than this at first but a number returned soon after the crisis and were reinitiated by the new guru. The matter is now largely forgotten, and is certainly of marginal significance in the 1983 and 1984 initiation figures.

Initiation   The process of initiation, which devotees undertake after at least a year of involvement in the movement, marks an important change. Before initiation a devotee could be said to be practising or rehearsing. If he or she fails to maintain the regulative principles (see Chapter Three), or wants to take a break from the lifestyle, they may

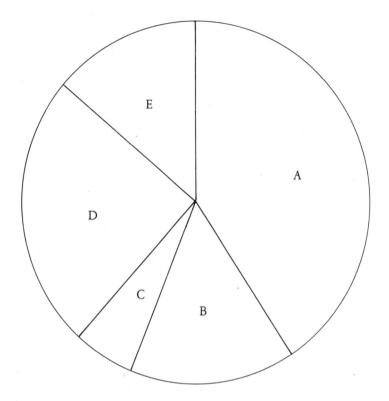

Trained devotees initiated in Britain between 1977 and 1984:

subsequent paths		per cent
A	Remain full-time in ISKCON (UK)	41
B	In ISKCON around the world	15
C	Left movement, or part-time	5
D	Left as a result of 1982 leadership problems	25
E	No information	14

The annual initiation totals reflect organizational changes in the movement. For example, in 1978 initiations were higher in number than the year before, 37 as compared with 24 in 1977. It was during 1977 that the introductory course was begun, and a major recruitment drive was undertaken in Central London (based at the Soho Street restaurant). Most of those attracted as a result of this would have taken initiation in 1978. Then in 1983, the year following the leadership changes, only 26 were initiated, compared to over 60 the previous year. The number has now risen again to 57 (1984) as a result of renewed stability within the movement.[6]

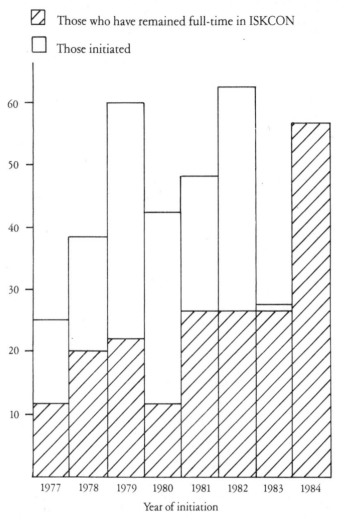

Trained devotees initiated in Britain between 1977 and 1984:
yearly totals and those who have remained full-time in ISKCON

These figures, for the full-time, initiated membership, although never
very high, do show that there has been a consistent attraction to the
lifestyle and philosophy offered at ISKCON centres in Britain. The
much-documented prophecy that the movement would be unlikely
to survive the death of the founder has not been vindicated.[7] *Instead*
a steady flow of interested people has continued to visit Bhaktivedanta
Manor as guests, trainees (bhaktas and bhaktins), and as potential
initiates.

do this of their own volition and there are no consequences. Initiation, however, consists of making vows and taking a new name. It is a rite of passage in which a new stage of life is reached. A bond of responsibility between the devotee and his or her spiritual master is formed which cannot be broken lightly. The vows are taken in order to be kept, not to be flaunted. This is why initiation is now given only to those who are ready to commit themselves fully to the discipline of Krishna Consciousness.

The 'Initiation into the Holy Name', as it is called, marks the first stage of full-time commitment. [8] After this ritual the devotees are said to have become either *brahmacharis* and *brahmacharins* (males and females respectively), or *grihastas*. The *brahmacharis* and *brahmacharins* are unmarried and celibate; the *grihastas* are married. These social categories correspond to traditional Indian stages of life (*ashramas*): the *brahmachari* is the young, celibate student, learning the religious texts and living an austere life; the *grihasta* is the householder. In the Hare Krishna movement these two groups can be distinguished by their appearance. The celibate male devotees wear saffron coloured clothes (*dhoti* and *kurta* or shirt), the married men wear white. All the women wear saris of various colours, but some married women make their status clear by wearing a red dot on their foreheads and a line of red make-up in the parting of their hair. Almost all the celibate devotees live in the Hare Krishna centres but most of the married devotees live in private houses nearby, attending all the temple services, eating many of their meals there, and often working either there or in local ISKCON places of work. Many of these couples have children who attend the primary school or the nursery at Bhaktivedanta Manor, live temporarily at the New Mayapur community in France and attend its high school, or spend their days with their mothers or their minders in the temple.

The life of a full-time devotee is one of devotional service irrespective of social status. All devotees chant the Hare Krishna mantra and work in the service of Krishna. Marriage is undertaken for bringing Krishna conscious children into the world. It is not an excuse for unbridled sex, however. The couple live together in order to support and protect one another, and to encourage one another in spiritual progress. These same functions are performed for the *brahmacharis* and *brahmacharins* by those in positions of authority, such as the temple president and his wife, and by their peers.

After a period of several years as a full-time initiated devotee one is entitled to be considered for '*brahmin* initiation'. Men and women, celibate or married, may undergo this ceremony, which then allows them to conduct religious services in the temple, to operate as a kind of priesthood. Subsequent to this stage it is possible for men, if they are considered suitable, to take *sannyasa,* a rite of renunciation. Only those who are felt to have developed a complete detachment from the trappings of material life are accepted. In fact, in India, *sannyasa* is taken generally by older men whose family responsibilities have been fulfilled. In the Hare Krishna movement, however, younger men become *sannyasis,* leaving their wives and children under the protection of a temple and its leaders. In this stage of life men are expected to be celibate and renounced. Their service is to preach to others and to enliven them in the process of spiritual progress. Because of the seriousness of this step, very few devotees have become *sannyasis.* Only one British devotee has ever taken *sannyasa.* He is now responsible for the movement in South-East Asia.

It used to be said that some men took this step because they had grown tired of their wives. Marriage was supposed to be 'for life', and renunciation seemed the only alternative. These days there appears to be more flexibility within the movement: if couples find it impossible to get on they will split up, one member usually leaving the temple and moving to another elsewhere. The principle, however, is one of no divorce, and all attempts are made by the spiritual master and other authorities to keep partners united. Unfortunately the same kinds of pressures and problems strike married couples in the movement as those outside it.

Renunciation is definitely not seen to be the solution to such troubles. *Sannyasa* not only involves the man leaving his wife and children for ever, but also the wife developing an equal spirit of detachment and purpose. The wives of *sannyasis* are considered as widows, paid great respect, and expected to be exemplary in their behaviour. The difference, of course, is that these women reach this stage informally. They do not undergo a ritual of renunciation. Both may agree that renunciation is the right path but the decision is generally centred around the man and not the woman.

The same rationale operates at most levels in the Hare Krishna movement because of its fundamental acceptance of the traditional Indian social system. Women can certainly take on positions of considerable responsibility. [9] They can devote themselves to a life of work should they want to. They can send their children to childminders and nurseries in order to continue their jobs. They can take *brahmin* initiation and can conduct daily religious services. They can give classes in the temple. What they must not do is to mix unnecessarily with men, particularly *sannyasis*, because for both sexes the objective is detachment from the temporary and illusory pleasures of material life and thus detachment from materially-based relationships with the opposite sex. Women, then, are to be avoided by men except in conjunction with mutual 'service', e.g. marriage, preaching and teaching activities, or an employment relationship. The opposite is also true. Men are to be avoided by women. In spiritual terms men and women are held to be equal. In human terms, however, women are understood to be in need of protection and shelter and, because in the traditional literature most of the issues are orientated towards celibate males, women are occasionally presented as something to be avoided. This unfortunately encourages some of the younger and less mature *brahmacharis* to look down on them. There are, of course, many married couples in the movement who are making a serious attempt to work out a relationship of mutual support and shared responsibility. This relationship is sought, however, within a philosophical context of male protection and female subservience.

Seen from the perspective of contemporary feminist attitudes the fundamental organization of the Hare Krishna movement is sexist although no more so than most of society's institutions. In terms of spiritual leadership, the orientation is generally male, although women are encouraged to take considerable practical responsibility. From the point of view of many of the devotees, the situation is acceptable and indeed appropriate. Feminism is not a major concern for most women and men within the movement, although there is an awareness amongst a growing number that the issue must be discussed and tackled if women are to continue to be attracted to the Krishna Consciousness movement.

In addition to this full-time membership, there are two other forms of commitment and interest in Krishna Consciousness. The Oxford Street chanters in their exotic apparel present the tradition of Chaitanya devotionalism for all to see and hear. Their aim is to spread 'a taste' for this religious form to their audience, to bring their faith to others. In this they have had considerable success, for despite the small numbers of those who have made a full-time commitment to the movement there are large numbers of people eager to participate in a more limited way in the principles and practices on offer. These people fall into two rather different groups, the Indian community — predominantly Hindu — with a foreknowledge of the cultural and religious background of *vaishnava bhakti* or devotion to Krishna, and a mixed group with an interest in such things as the literature and the meditational qualities of chanting but a firm desire to remain in their current social, geographical and occupational locations. For both these groups Krishna Consciousness, the practices which fuel and express it, and the beliefs which are an intrinsic part of it, constitute one aspect of a life comprised also of work, family, friends, sport, and leisure. Just as there are those for whom church attendance and Christian prayer are an integral part of ordinary life, so there are those for whom Krishna Consciousness functions in the same way. Some may even be combining the two, an acceptance of the basic tenets of Christianity with an interest in Hare Krishna belief and practice. The Indian Hindus similarly combine a number of complex religious allegiances. Many continue to attend local temples and to worship a number of different deities (Shiva, Durga, Rama, Ganesh and Hanuman) and saints (such as Sai Baba). They also make special trips to the Hare Krishna centres to pay their obeisances to Krishna, to take *prasadam*, and to buy books in English, Hindi, Gujarati, or Bengali.

The Friends of Lord Krishna (FOLK) In recent years, as the movement has become more established and its members more mature, there has been a gradual move away from the frenetic urge to 'engage' people in the full-time service of Krishna to a more socially informed desire to tempt them without demanding an immediate change in lifestyle. The Indian Hindu population has built up a complex relationship with the Hare Krishna devotees which suits its own particular needs and requirements. Those who do not have a cultural and religious affinity with the Hindu beliefs and practices of the movement — largely the indigenous population but also some West Indians, Africans, and members of other ethnic minorities recently settled in the UK — have traditionally been harder to attract to Krishna Consciousness.

Two initiatives in particular have been responsible for building up a community of interested non-Hindu lay persons. The first, started in Britain in about 1979, was the mail order business dealing in books, incense, etc., which maintained contacts with interested people all over the country. This business is able to organize the supply of such items to destinations throughout Britain and to maintain an up-to-date address list of those currently interested in the movement, its literature and its lifestyle. At present there are about 5,000 names on the list, which is growing at a rate of 10 per cent a year.

It was this mail order system that enabled the second of the two initiatives to be put into operation in January 1981. In that month ISKCON (UK) produced its first edition of *Folk Magazine,* a quarterly publication designed for the 'Friends of Lord Krishna' (FOLK). The monthly *Back to Godhead* magazine was still produced in the United States and distributed internationally, but this new journal was designed to speak more directly to a British audience, specifically to a British audience with its roots firmly fixed in ordinary life. There was an awareness amongst the leadership that an influx of full-time devotees into community life would create serious problems. How would they be housed and fed? Where would they be employed? Instead, it was envisaged that growth in the movement would be of a different nature:

> The vast majority of people would be remaining in their houses, keeping their jobs, thus continuing economic self-sufficiency . . . Ultimately we want to have people who, although not living in a temple, represent Krishna consciousness in whatever they do, and wherever they go. They are more likely to be able to preach by *not* giving up their family and, by continuing to live in a neighbourhood of non-devotees, people will be more apt to relate to them. [*Folk Magazine*, 1:1, 1981, pp. 4-5]

The magazine was aimed at such people and designed to stimulate their interest in and commitment to the principles and practices of Krishna Consciousness in conjunction with ordinary working life and family life. Its style and content reflected these objectives, and articles covered such issues as contemporary political and social concerns, guidance in practising the principles of the movement, philosophical matters such as karma and reincarnation, personal profiles of leaders, devotees and FOLK members, and the words of the founder, Prabhupada.

The content portrayed a clear picture of the movement's expectations of a life of Krishna Consciousness 'out there' in society. It was not expected to be easy: members were encouraged to visit the centres, to write in to the magazine with problems and suggestions, and to organize local meetings with other FOLK members. Further commitment and new initiatives were naturally welcomed: members could distribute literature to friends and neighbours; they could suggest business schemes; enrol on the introductory training programme; make regular financial donations, or even become ISKCON life members.

Only a few of those who received *Folk Magazine* went on to this level of commitment although a number adopted the recommended daily practices of chanting, worship and offering food to Krishna, and developed a more detailed knowledge of the philosophy of the movement. The current distribution policy is designed to cater for more serious congregational members rather than all those on the mailing list.

Other strategies have been developed in order to work with this section of the membership. Chanting and preaching in Central London continue to attract a small number of people, and the sale and distribution of books and paintings in southern England provide new contacts. Recent schemes initiated to follow up these contacts and establish new ones come under the heading of 'contact *sankirtana*'. This general policy, instigated in 1984, proceeds from the premise that messages are best communicated between friends. This means, on the one hand, that friendship networks provide perhaps the most reliable method for spreading Krishna Consciousness, and, on the other, that if devotees develop close friendships with interested outsiders they will help to fuel their spiritual lives. In one scheme resulting from this a national survey of mailing list members has been undertaken in order to ascertain their depth of commitment to the movement.

Other schemes which fall under the general heading of contact *sankirtana* are the V.I.P. programme and the university programme. The first is a campaign whereby well-known and well-established people from various walks of life are 'cultivated' by the more socially able of the devotees. There is already a substantial number of famous personalities with an interest in the movement who are encouraged to bring their friends and families to the headquarters at Bhaktivedanta Manor for Indian (*Vedic*) dinner parties, and audiences with the guru. [10]

As young people have been the main source for recruitment since the earliest days of Hare Krishna, universities and colleges have always been a target for the movement's preaching. The emphasis now, though, is on the more personal approach and on building up and sustaining contacts — for instance, through evening classes, which do not have to be formal philosophy sessions: vegetarian cookery classes provide as good an opportunity for the discussion of Krishna Consciousness lifestyle and beliefs, but in a less intense and serious framework. The aim is not so much to convert students and discourage them from their studies and future careers as to stimulate their interest in questions concerning spirituality.

In recent years the Bhaktivedanta Book Trust has developed a policy for reaching a wider audience, through libraries, bookshops, and schools. The Book Trust has established itself with major sales outlets and has a close relationship with the Inner London Education Authority, which encourages its schools to buy books with a multi-cultural and multi-religious educational approach. 'Bala Books', the children's publications produced by the Book Trust, tell stories about India, her deities and way of life. In conjunction with the Book Trust's tapes, slides, and posters, these books are seen by many teachers and educational advisors as helping to meet the needs of a multi-faith school intake and a multi-cultural curriculum. One of the reasons for this success is the absence in Britain of a resource base for Hinduism comparable to the educational services provided by some of the other religious communities. ISKCON has worked closely with the National Council of Hindu Temples to meet this need.

Much effort has been expended by the movement in bringing the indigenous British population to Krishna Consciousness: one of the movement's leaders has stated that Hare Krishna has contributed quite considerably to the contemporary upsurge of interest in the idea of reincarnation and the practice of vegetarianism. [11] Although these have also been brought to our notice by other cultural routes, the Hare Krishna movement has certainly lent weight to their popularity. Both reincarnation and vegetarianism, of course, have their oldest roots in India, and there is thus a natural affinity between the Hare Krishna movement and the Indian community.

The Indian Community   It is assumed by many commentators on 'new religions' that their members are almost totally young and white. For the Hare Krishna movement this is not the case. [12] Certainly most of the full-time devotees in this country fall into this category, although an increasing number are black. The FOLK membership, too, is predominantly indigenous. However, the largest show of support and interest in Britain for the principles and practices of Krishna Consciousness comes from the Indian community, almost exclusively from the Hindu population.

The Hindus, like the Muslims and the Sikhs, have been settling and developing communities in Britain since the 1950s. The largest influx of their number, however, arrived between 1965 and 1973 from East Africa, where they had been settled for many years and were engaged in trade and industry. [13] There are currently in excess of 300,000 Indian Hindus living in Britain. Most of them are of Gujarati origin; that is to say, they were either born in Gujarat State in the West of India or claim linguistic and cultural identity with that region and its people. Nearly a third of the Hindus are Punjabis, and a small number originate from other Indian regions such as Maharashtra, Bengal, or Tamil Nadu.

The majority of these Hindus practise their religion at home and, during festival periods, in the Hindu temples in Britain's cities. Most families have their own traditional deity, who might be the elephant-headed god Ganesh, Shiva, Hanuman the monkey god who gave his support to Rama in his fight against the demon Ravana, or the goddess Mataji (otherwise known as Ambamata or Durga). Daily worship of the family deity is carried out at home, but special religious occasions involve more social celebrations. At these times most families visit their local Hindu temples and centres, of which there are about a hundred in Britain. Some of these places of worship (*mandirs*) are sectarian: they are aligned to particular Hindu movements such as the *Satya Sai Baba* organization or the *Swaminarayan* movement. The majority are what is most commonly described as *sanatana dharma* temples. It would be wrong to call these 'orthodox' Hindu temples, and the others 'unorthodox', as the notion of orthodoxy makes very little sense in a broad and all-embracing faith like Hinduism. *Sanatana dharma*, however, is generally understood to mean 'eternal tradition', and most Hindus see it as describing the correct and authentic philosophy and practice of their religion. In addition, most of these *sanatana dharma* temples contain ceremonially installed images (*murtis*) of Krishna and his consort, Radha, the most popular and universally known of the Hindu deities.

It is against this background that the relationship between ISKCON and the Indian community has been established. All Britain's Indian Hindus recognize the religion and culture of the Hare Krishna devotees. They see it as similar to their own (and thus a legitimate expression of *sanatana dharma*) except in so far as it is generally practised with greater commitment, greater austerity, and greater philosophical awareness. The vast majority of Indian Hindus have a profound respect for the devotees; there is no feeling amongst them that this is not 'real' Hinduism, or that the devotees are 'playing' at Indian religion and culture. To many, the Hare Krishna devotees, unlike the members of other new Eastern-based religious groups, are the true exemplars of Hinduism in its new geographical location. [14]

It is for these reasons that from the very earliest days of the Hare Krishna movement in Britain Indians have been eager to associate with the devotees and give financial help. In 1969, when Bhaktivedanta Swami Prabhupada first came to England his public lectures were attended not just by students and hippies but also by Indians: in fact, he had not been able to preach so extensively to Indians since he had lived in India in the early 1960s, and when the Bury Place temple was being prepared for worship, an Indian Hindu society donated images of Radha and Krishna for installation as deities. [15]

This close relationship has continued through the 1970s and 1980s. Every Sunday large numbers visit the main temple at Bhaktivedanta Manor outside Watford, from Hindu communities as far afield as Lancashire, West Yorkshire, the West Midlands, and South Wales. On some Sundays the afternoon and evening programmes can attract as many as 1,500 Hindu visitors, whilst during the two-day celebration of Lord Krishna's birthday (*Janamashtami*) some 25,000 people go to Bhaktivedanta Manor to worship Krishna and to celebrate his anniversary. [16]

The relationship between the Hare Krishna movement and the Indian Hindu community is thus a well-established one. The Indians offer their financial support and show a genuine and sustained desire to use the services of ISKCON, to visit its centres, to make use of its priests (*pujaris*, who have undergone *brahmin* initiation and been trained to offer to the deities) in conducting worship and in performing marriages in homes and temples throughout the country, and to meet with and work alongside the devotees. Some take a more serious interest in the movement, and become initiated members. [17] In exchange, ISKCON provides services and facilities in conjunction with what is known as the Indian Community Affairs Programme. Regular weekly and annual events are organized, youth clubs for Indian children are provided, and Indian cultural events are run. An ISKCON temple and restaurant has recently opened in the main Indian shopping street in Leicester which operates in close contact with the large Gujarati Hindu population there. Two other examples illustrate the scope and nature of this relationship. One is the magazine sponsored and printed by ISKCON but compiled by a mixed group of Indian Hindus and full-time devotees, the *Mahabharat Times*. The other is the National Council of Hindu Temples, of which ISKCON is a member. As a member of the NCHT, with representation on its general committee and its public relations sub-committee, it is concerned with what has recently been described as an initiative for the 'unity and consolidation' of Hinduism in Britain. [18] The NCHT, which represents over thirty-five of the largest Hindu temples in Britain, has consistently stood by the Hare Krishna movement against attacks on it as a new and supposedly dangerous cult. Many Hindus feel that when the Hare Krishna movement is described in these terms the religion of a third of Britain's South Asian population is being attacked. To them, Krishna Consciousness is a genuine form of Hinduism, and the Hare Krishna devotees are sincere *vaishnavas*. Hinduism is not a cult but a world religion of great antiquity; *vaishnavism* is not a brainwashing technique but a form of worship and belief adhered to by Hindus throughout India and in Indian communities the world over.

3

The Beliefs and Practices
of Krishna Consciousness

What attracts people to the Hare Krishna movement? One person might turn to Krishna Consciousness because of a radical disenchantment with the values and attitudes that underlie contemporary life; another might join after experiencing a personal trauma. Generally speaking, part of the incentive for joining is provided by negative feelings towards the current state of one's own life. However, dissatisfaction or frustration, inertia or alienation, are not enough to explain the dramatic step the devotee takes in leaving one life for another.

There is a positive attraction as well. Something, or many things, within the philosophy and lifestyle of the movement makes the step seem worthwhile, even irresistible.

(i) *The Philosophy of Krishna Consciousness*   Unlike some new religious and meditational groups, which offer only a very general theory of human life and a series of techniques for coping with it, the Hare Krishna movement, because of its origins, offers a complete cosmological, philosophical, and social system. Indian religion has a recorded history of some four thousand years, and even though Chaitanya Mahaprabhu, the earliest exponent of the particular form of devotionalism of today's Hare Krishna movement, lived only five hundred years ago, the roots of his religious contribution go back much further. *Vaishnavism* is practised throughout India, and Krishna Consciousness is an important *Vaishnava* movement. As already indicated, Indians throughout the world recognize these beliefs and practices as authentic aspects of Indian religious tradition. Krishna is worshipped by millions and many others serve Vishnu or Rama, both of whom are associated with Krishna. All Indians are conversant with the religious terminology used by the movement: concepts like *karma, dharma, avatara, samsara, maya, moksha, ashrama, varna,* and *bhakti* are Hindu concepts, used by them in religious and philosophical contexts when Christians might talk about such things as free will and predestination, resurrection, faith, salvation, grace, and the love of God. [1] Not least of all, all Hindus share a respect for the most widely-known and popular of Indian religious texts, the *Bhagavad Gita*, the central text of the Hare Krishna movement.

Prabhupada's own translation and commentary, *Bhagavad-gita As It Is* is read by all the members. There is a long-standing tradition in India of *Gita* commentaries. Many scholars have contributed to this tradition, including the early philosophers Sankara, Ramanuja and Madhva, and more recent commentators such as the Indian nationalist leader B. G. Tilak and the founder of the Transcendental Meditation movement, Maharishi Mahesh Yogi. Like any religious text the *Bhagavad Gita* has been open to a wide range of interpretations. To the Hare Krishna devotees Prabhupada's presentation is the most authentic, since he was himself a devotee of Krishna and a guru in the spiritual lineage of Chaitanya Mahaprabhu, and hence of Krishna Himself. [2]

The *Bhagavad-gita As It Is* provides a framework for understanding the philosophy of Krishna Consciousness. It is a philosophy which, while having much in common with popular Hinduism, distinguishes itself from the mainstream by focusing on the notion of 'consciousness'. According to the Hare Krishna movement, popular Hinduism, with its many gods and goddesses and its emphasis on pragmatism, has become empty of meaning for people because it is not answering their spiritual needs in a way they can respond to. Its message is not strong enough to arouse its adherents from lethargy and attachment to the material world. The Hare Krishna movement however, like the whole Krishna *bhakti* tradition before it, seeks to make people aware of their relation to God, and to fuel this relationship constantly. The *Bhagavad Gita*, according to Prabhupada, does just this. It tells the story of one man's relationship with Lord Krishna. Using the example of this man, Arjuna, Krishna shows His devotees how to live both in service to Him and in consciousness of Him. It is thus said to be 'the science of Krishna' [Prabhupada, 1973, p. 87].

But how can the *Bhagavad Gita* be called 'a science'? And what might be said to constitute this 'science of Krishna' which so attracts devotees to give their lives in service? The *Bhagavad Gita*, according to Prabhupada, provides an account and explanation of the way things really are — the nature of God, the 'spirit-soul', and the material world — and a method or path for gaining insight into the purpose of these things, and thus for fulfilling that purpose.

God and the soul　In Chapter Eleven of the *Gita* there is a powerful description of Krishna Himself. He appears to Arjuna because, as Arjuna's teacher as well as God Himself, He wants to guide him to realization. This theophany of Krishna's 'universal form' shows Him as awesome and all-powerful, as frightening and unlimited, but, as His relationship with Arjuna has previously shown, He is also loving, approachable, and merciful.

Krishna is considered by Prabhupada to be 'the supreme personality of Godhead'. He is a personal God with whom we have a relationship. The fact that we are related to him in this way does not detract from His supremacy, however. He is unlimited and ultimately unfathomable. At times, though, He manifests Himself in a shape and form we can understand. For example, He appeared at different times as Rama, the Buddha, and Lord Chaitanya (three of his incarnations or *avataras*). He is all-attractive because by virtue of His many roles He can win the hearts of everyone. Ordinary mortals, even though they are in reality 'spirit-souls', are so attached to the material world that they cannot be expected to appreciate 'Godhead', Krishna in His perfect state. So in order to attract these souls 'back home, back to Godhead', Krishna must turn them away from the material world and point them in the right direction. This explains why He appears in many incarnations or *avataras*.

The supreme Krishna is not limited by His original form of the flute-playing cowherder. He is using His all-attractive form as a means to win the devotees' hearts, and thus to enliven and enlighten them in their search for truth. The form and personality of God or Krishna are not limited to this particular role, or to the role of counselling charioteer in the *Bhagavad Gita*. They are not limited to this incarnation, the one we commonly call 'Krishna', just as they are not limited to the incarnation called 'Rama' or 'the Buddha'. The ultimate form and personality of Godhead cannot be understood by inductive or subjective reasoning. It is described to us — in the theophany of the *Gita*, and in the testimony of the *Vishnu Purana* — but we cannot grasp these descriptions because our understanding is limited by material definitions. Human beings can only appreciate Krishna when, by His mercy, He appears to be less than He really is. [3]

Most importantly, Krishna is a personal God, not an impersonal force. This is wholly different from what Prabhupada called the 'impersonalist' philosophy, the doctrine of Absolute Oneness, of an absolute identification or non-difference between the supreme force (*brahman*) and the individual spirit (*atman*). This view, described in the early *Upanishads*, and taken up by Sankara in the ninth century, had become popular in intellectual circles in India and amongst seekers in the West by the time Prabhupada was writing. He saw it as misguided because it hindered people from following the path of truth, *bhakti-yoga*, the way of devotion through service. According to Prabhupada, the individual souls were not just God by any other name. As he put it, they were not just rivers joining an ocean, to lose their individual identity forever and to be, not just a part of the ocean, but the ocean itself. Instead they were more like the creatures that live in the sea, participating in ocean-life and enjoying it but separate from the sea itself which supported them. [4] The individual soul was 'part and parcel' of Krishna, like a spark from a fire [Prabhupada, 1977, p. 50]. It was of the same nature, but separate from God. The spirit souls have fallen from the fire — from Krishna, their original home — into material bondage, into the bodies of women and men, plants and animals. The aim, then, is to use life for the re-establishment of the original relationship of soul and God, of *jiva* and Krishna.

The material world   Our real self, then, is the soul which inhabits the body and gives it life. The soul is eternal; the body is impermanent and life is transitory. After a life in this body the soul will take life again in another. It will transmigrate, experiencing life again and again until such time as it returns to Krishna. The soul is not 'reborn' as such, but the body in which it finds itself is born, ages, and dies. It is of this material world, and like the material world it is *maya*, or illusion. This is a familiar Indian concept but one which has been interpreted in many different ways. To Prabhupada *maya* is the illusory energy responsible for deluding people about their real spiritual nature. *Maya* gets in the way of self-realization. It captivates people, encourages them to identify themselves with their material bodies, and hence binds them to the pursuit of material goals.

The life resulting from this captivation with *maya* is unsatisfying. Most obviously, it is bound to end. Death cannot be avoided. In addition, life itself is full of suffering: pleasure, happiness, and success are just round the corner but never stay for long. Even if a person finds a life of contentment, how can this be squared with the inevitable process of ageing and dying in oneself and others?

Maya, or material energy, also bears a relationship to Krishna. According to Prabhupada there are two kinds of energy, material and spiritual energy. Both 'rest' on Krishna but neither 'is' Krishna (Prabhupada, 1973, Chapter Three). Krishna is 'everywhere present' but none of the things which are a part of His energy (the souls which are a part of His spiritual energy or the bodies which are in some sense a part of His material energy) can be said to be Krishna. Krishna is more than the sum of His parts.

Even though our real nature is spiritual and we are trapped in the material world, we should act as though our bodies and minds are neither our friends nor our enemies. We should treat them as neither good nor bad. They are only what we, through our actions and attitudes, make them. The soul, despite being eternal and having the potential for Krishna Consciousness, has to cope with luggage on its journeys through material nature. And this luggage, the product of *karma* or past actions, determines what happens to it each time it takes birth. From the way Prabhupada describes this process of rebirth (generally referred to as *samsara*) it seems it is not so much that at this time the soul carries its own luggage but that a porter, the subtle body, carries it instead, at the same time selecting a destination which seems appropriate to the nature of the luggage:

> After the destruction of the gross body, which is made up of the senses, blood, bone, fat, and so forth, the subtle body of mind, intelligence, and ego goes on working. So at the time of death this subtle body carries the small spirit soul to another gross body . . . According to the condition of the mind at the time of death, the minute spirit soul enters into the womb of a particular mother through the semen of a father, and then the soul develops a particular type of body given by the mother. It may be a human being, it may be a cat, a dog, or anything. [Prabhupada, 1977, pp. 28-9]

The luggage is the product of *karma,* a law to which we are all subject, a law of cause and effect. Prabhupada, in common with the majority of Indian religious teachers, stressed this principle. The way we choose to live now, in this life, will determine our fate in the next. This will be ensured, as he states, by 'the condition of the mind at the time of death'. So, the soul may well be meant for better things, indeed for a life of devotion to Krishna, but it may not necessarily be given the opportunity it needs to pursue its intended path. Prabhupada's most persistent message was that material self-gratification for its own sake would result in unwelcome luggage and continued suffering in the round of birth and death. The alternative, the pursuit of an awareness of the real state of things and consequent life of love and service to Krishna, would result in an end to birth and death, to the sorrows of material existence.

A basic principle of this new consciousness, according to Prabhupada and repeated again and again in the early chapters of the *Bhagavad Gita*, is that we should change our attitude to the things we do. Things must be done, not for the rewards they promise to bring, but without desire for exploiting these results. We must continue to live and work in the material world but we must not strive only after material ends. To do so will bring us unhappiness in the future either in this life or the next, and probably both. Instead we must continue to act according to our position in life, as Krishna recommends Arjuna to do, and must develop a spirit of detachment. Only then can the fire of material life cease to burn us, and only then can we begin to bring an end to the cycle of birth and death.

The path to realization   Bringing an end to the karmic cycle is clearly desirable, but when viewed in relation to the difficulty of the path it seems almost unattainable; and besides, life contains pleasure as well as pain. It was in order to attract those who might fall at this first hurdle in the quest for liberation that Krishna in the *Bhagavad Gita* spoke of *bhakti*. Prabhupada, like those before him in the Chaitanya tradition, made this the centre of his philosophy. The goal to be sought was not simply the ending of suffering: it was also the pursuit of love, along a path of love. Liberation (*moksha*) should not be strived after for its own sake, any more than material gratification. Prabhupada, reiterating Krishna's own advice in the *Gita*, recommends *bhakti-yoga*, or the path of devotion, to those who want to develop their spiritual selves. This path, in addition to leading its followers away from material life, brings the joy which attends a loving relationship.

In the *Bhagavad Gita* Krishna Himself admits there are other paths to realization. There is the way of action, *karma-yoga*, and the path of knowledge, *jnana-yoga*. In common with the majority of commentators Prabhupada sees these as lesser paths than the way of devotion or *bhakti*. Work and wisdom (*karma* and *jnana*) are part of any path to realization, but to concentrate on one of these shuts our eyes to Krishna and the loving relationship He offers. Social work or intellectual effort make sense only if they are part of a pursuit of Krishna Consciousness.

Bhakti-yoga is also the easiest of all the paths to God open to us. In perhaps the most oft-quoted verse of the *Bhagavad-Gita* Krishna says, 'If one offers Me with love and devotion a leaf, a flower, fruit or water, I will accept it.' [*Bhagavad-gita As It Is*, 9: 26; Prabhupada, 1972, p. 478.] It is not necessary to renounce everything; all that is necesary is love and devotion, of which everyone is capable. Even a simple act of offering is transformed into a meaningful interaction with Krishna: the devotee offers; Krishna accepts. Krishna goes on to say, 'Engage your mind always in thinking of Me, become my devotee, offer obeisances and worship Me. Being completely absorbed in Me, surely you will come to Me.' [*Bhagavad-gita As It Is*, 9: 34; Prabhupada, 1972, p. 489.]

This explains a great deal of the philosophy and lifestyle of the Hare

Krishna movement. Prabhupada constantly reiterated the notion of 'devotional service'. Nothing was to be done except with Krishna in mind: chanting, offering food, worship, sweeping-up, gardening, procreating. Everything was for Him. But, as he had realized from his own experience and from the writings of those in the Chaitanya tradition before him, even devotional service focused on Krishna was difficult. How could people be guided *practically* towards Krishna Consciousness? How could *bhakti* even begin to make sense for people who were bound so tightly to material possessions and transitory goals?

The answer was simple. It was not Prabhupada's own idea. Like all his teachings it came from what to him was an authoritative source, from his teacher and those before him in the line of disciplic succession. In fact, it was just that, the concept of the *guru*. Again, Prabhupada uses an illustration from the *Bhagavad Gita,* this time to show how the seeker should ask for help and guidance from one who is qualified. Arjuna, who at the beginning of the battle is overwhelmed with despair at the prospect of fighting his kin, speaks to Krishna as one who needs such help and guidance: 'Now I am confused about my duty and have lost all composure because of weakness. In this condition I am asking You to tell me clearly what is best for me. Now I am your disciple and a soul surrendered unto You. Please instruct me.' [*Bhagavad-gita As It Is*, 2: 7; Prabhupada, 1972, p. 79.]

Arjuna took Krishna, his friend and charioteer, as his guru. Likewise, Prabhupada recommended all serious seekers to do the same. [5] It is for this reason that, before his death, he gave the responsibility for initiation to some of the devotees who had made most progress in Krishna Consciousness. He was always quite clear on the relationship of the guru to Krishna, however. The guru is not God, but he is to be shown respect in the way God would be shown respect. The guru takes the position (*pada*) of the Lord (*prabhu*) here and now (hence, *prabhupada*), and should thus be treated accordingly (Prabhupada, 1977, p. 59). He is the servant of Krishna, however, just as his own disciples are. [6]

Prabhupada laid down very clear guidelines on how to proceed towards self-realization. Finding a guru was one of the first steps, but other principles and practices were also important. Devotional service, chanting the names of God, bringing Krishna Consciousness to the attention of others, caring for the deities, vigilance, cleanliness, austerity — all these things were seen as intrinsic to *bhakti-yoga* and thus to Krishna consciousness. These issues are discussed at length in his books, particularly in the short instructive handbooks such as *The Perfection of Yoga* and *Raja Vidya: The King of Knowledge*, and in his lectures and classes, many of which are printed in *Back to Godhead* magazine and compiled in the volume entitled *The Science of Self-Realisation*. As these books show, the real essence of *bhakti-yoga* is not the 'contemplation' of love of Krishna but the 'practice' of love of Krishna.

(ii) *The Practice of Krishna Consciousness*   As we saw in the last chapter, the significant event that distinguishes the more casual seeker from the fully committed devotee is the ceremony of initiation. It is this event which binds the disciple to the guru for life, and which marks the beginning of a serious commitment to the principles of Krishna Consciousness. The guru not only becomes responsible for the instruction of the disciple, but also takes on the effects of this person's actions. The *karma* of the disciple is henceforth absorbed by the guru. In exchange, the devotee promises to practise the minimum requirements of a life of true Krishna consciousness. These requirements are: that the devotee should keep the four regulative principles — that is, that he or she should eat no meat, fish or eggs, consume no intoxicants, not indulge in illicit sex, and refrain from gambling; in addition, he or she vows to chant sixteen 'rounds' on *japa* beads each day, and to read for an hour from the works of Bhaktivedanta Swami Prabhupada. The final, and most important requirement, is devotional service.

Once these vows are made the devotee receives a new, spiritual name. Each name is comprised of an initial part, such as 'Chaitanyacharana' (the feet of Lord Chaitanya) or 'Rohininandana' (the son of Rohini), after which follows a suffix meaning 'servant'. A female devotee would then become known as 'Chaitanyacharana devi dasi', 'devi' meaning 'goddess', and 'dasi', 'servant'. A male devotee takes the addition 'dasa'. A devotee with the name 'Rohininandana dasa' is therefore called 'the servant of the son of Rohini'.

The initiation of the disciple by the guru is complete when the guru gives the new initiate a set of *japa* beads on which he has previously chanted the Hare Krishna mantra. The devotee is now fixed in a permanent relationship with the guru, and has also taken on the outward sign of an eternal relationship to Krishna, as His 'servant'.

Regulation and self-discipline   Service to God can take many forms, but all forms of service are better conducted if one is in a clean, healthy, and self-disciplined state of being. This is almost the first thing a devotee learns in Krishna Consciousness: those who join the introductory training programme find themselves abruptly shaken from their previous routines and habits and confronted with a very different daily ritual. Early rising, invigorating showers, no sex, a bunk bed in a shared room, and a life of chanting, worship and service — these are the features of the new lifestyle. Austerity is not valued for its own sake. It is necessary because of the nature of material life and the further problems brought on by the age in which we now live. Material life is impermanent. It brings pain and suffering. Bacon and eggs, alcohol, and frivolous sex might give a few moments of pleasure but the new devotees are reminded of the pig's right to life, the aggression brought on by alcohol, the anxieties brought on by 'sleeping around'. Moreover, indulging in the trappings of material existence only binds one still further to such an existence, and hinders one from seeing its folly. If a devotee desires to find eternal happiness with Krishna a radical break with such impermanent pleasures is necessary. It is a question of choosing the 'greater good'.

Every devotee refrains from eating meat, fish and eggs, and instead consumes a diet of vegetables, pulses, fruit, grains, and milk products. No devotee must touch alcohol, tea, or coffee; decaffeinated versions, fruit juice, herb teas and milk drinks are substituted. Drugs are also prohibited, and the movement earned considerable respect in its early days for the way it helped young people who had turned to marijuana, LSD, cocaine and other drugs to give up their addiction.

The next principle is the regulation of sex. The bulk of initiated devotees are either *brahmacharis* or *grihastas,* celibate students or married householders. When the devotees vow to give up 'illicit sex' at the initiation ceremony they understand that sex should only occur within marriage, for the procreation of children. Questions about contraception and abortion, therefore, do not arise within the movement. Sex, like any other aspect of material existence, is not to be enjoyed for its own sake but because of the way in which, within marriage, it can be used to serve Krishna. Bringing children into a world of Krishna Consciousness is seen to be an important part of devotional service.

Finally, the devotees must not engage in any kind of gambling, which includes financial investments of a speculative variety as well as backing horses, playing cards, bingo, and so on.

Chanting Each initiated devotee is expected to chant the Hare Krishna mantra for at least an hour and a half each day. The chanting is done on a string of *japa* beads. There are 108 beads in total on which the devotee chants the mantra, and the whole process must be repeated sixteen times a day. The short verse, 'Hare Krishna Hare Krishna, Krishna Krishna Hare Hare, Hare Rama Hare Rama, Rama Rama Hare Hare', is therefore chanted a total of 1,728 times per day.

As we saw in Chapter One, the *maha mantra* represents the names of God. Chanting this mantra is felt to be both meditational and devotional because it serves to calm the mind and body of the devotee as well as to bring them into a relationship with Krishna in which they are empowered to serve Him. Chanting the holy name (*namajapa*) allows the devotee to associate with Krishna, and therefore to purify their consciousness while, at the same time, asking to be engaged in devotional service. For these reasons the chanting is generally done early in the morning so that its benefits may be felt during the day's work. Chanting thus has both a mystical and an active purpose.

Kirtana, in which the names of God are not chanted but sung, often to an accompaniment of musical instruments, clapping and dancing, takes place daily as part of the regular schedule of worship. Again, the benefits are felt to be physical as well as spiritual. Singing and dancing have a therapeutic effect, whilst to be 'ecstatic' in song and dance is to be fully caught up in the mood of devotion to Krishna.

Scholarship It is not necessary to demand that devotees make a vow to sing and dance. By and large this comes naturally. Steps are taken, however, to ensure that they educate themselves in the teachings of the movement. At the initiation ceremony each devotee vows to read for an hour a day from the many works of Bhaktivedanta Swami Prabhupada, from his translations of the *Bhagavad Gita* or the *Bhagavata Purana* or the *Caitanya-caritamrta,* from his expositions of the path of Krishna Consciousness, from his lectures or letters.

This commitment to study is made possible by the fact that the majority of Prabhupada's works, despite his Bengali background, were written in English. In choosing this medium he was following the instructions of his own spiritual master, Bhaktisiddhanta Saraswati Goswami, whose plan it was to make Chaitanya devotionalism available to the West. The printed word was seen to be the key to success in preaching, particularly in the West, and Prabhupada as a consequence spent years translating the devotional texts of the *bhakti* tradition, and writing commentaries, discourses, letters, and essays in English.

Though the English language was seen to be the medium by which people in the West could be brought to an understanding of Krishna Consciousness, Sanskrit was the sacred language of *Vedic* knowledge. It is for this reason that English has not taken over as the liturgical language of the movement. The songs, prayers, and scriptural readings continue to be sung, recited, and read in Sanskrit (or Bengali, when they are from a later historical period).

Prabhupada was careful to convey Krishna *bhakti* just as he had received it from his own spiritual master; his devotees and the devotees of the gurus who have succeeded him are eager to do the same. The

The spiritual master leading a *kirtana*.

spiritual succession, as the devotees see it, is the vital link between Krishna Consciousness today and the *Vedic* past. To deviate from the tradition is to endanger the individual spiritual quest and the message of the movement itself.[7] The history of ISKCON is littered with debates in which devotees have interpreted aspects of philosophy or practice in controversial ways and have been chastised for it.[8] There is a straight and narrow path in Krishna Consciousness to which devotees must adhere. It was to avoid the destructive consequences of internal dissent that Prabhupada invested both the Governing Body Commission and the initiating gurus with the power to succeed him. It is for the same reason that all devotees are charged with the personal responsibility of reading and hearing the philosophy passed down through the disciplic succession of gurus and written down in English by Prabhupada.

Service and worship Initiated devotees are also expected to attend a daily class generally given by a senior devotee.[9] These duties constitute part of the daily programme of service and worship.

At Bhaktivedanta Manor the day begins at about four o'clock in the morning when the devotees — adults and children alike — rise, shower, and prepare themselves. They then assemble in the temple at 4.30 for *Mangalarti,* the first religious service of the day. On the way in, after removing their shoes, they pay their obeisances. They are now in the presence of the deities. At this time of day Radha and Krishna, Rama, Sita, Lakshman and Hanuman (the deities at Bhaktivedanta Manor) are still in their night clothes. Each day they are bathed, dressed, and offered food and water, light, incense, and flowers by the temple priest or *pujari* and worshipped by the devotees. *Mangalarti* provides the first opportunity of the day for the devotees to see the deities.[10] After this they spend nearly two hours chanting the *maha mantra*. This time, from about 5.15 to 7.00, is known as the '*japa* period'. At 7.00 the devotees congregate in the temple to greet the deities and make offerings to the guru in the daily *Guru Puja.*[11] By this time the deities have been dressed in their day clothes and after singing songs to Krishna, Prabhupada, and the current spiritual master, and offering flowers, the devotees sit down to listen to the daily lecture, in which the speaker takes a verse from scripture and discusses its implications for spiritual life. This is followed by a short session in which the devotees are given an opportunity to ask questions of the speaker.

Before the devotees leave the temple for their day's work (known as 'service') they take *prasadam*, a meal comprised of food which has been offered to Krishna. Because this is the only occasion when all the devotees meet together, they eat their main meal of the day at this

Devotees at worship. (J. Shorthouse).

time (8.30-9.30). The kinds of service in which the devotees are engaged are many and various — from teaching, cooking, and gardening to distributing books and food. *Sankirtana*, the name given to those activities which help to spread Chaitanya Mahaprabhu's devotional movement, takes a number of forms. The members of the Central London chanting party, who sing the Hare Krishna mantra and dance in the streets, are engaged in *sankirtana*. The devotees who stand in town centres and give books in exchange for donations are also engaged in *sankirtana*. So are those who sell paintings door-to-door, or distribute food, or give vegetarian cookery classes, or talk to interested families, school parties, and college groups. All of this work helps to put people in touch with Krishna Consciousness and is seen as being vital to the movement.

Devotee working in a garden. (J. Shorthouse).

Of all the forms of *sankirtana*, the most beneficial to the devotee and to ISKCON as a whole is considered to be the one in which the devotee not only seeks to raise funds but attempts to engage the donor in the service of Krishna. Selling books or paintings is only possible if the devotee is fully committed to serving Krishna and the spiritual master, and is thus fully prepared to encounter a range of adverse responses. The task of going from door-to-door, or stopping strangers in the street, is one which requires humility and perseverance, but the devotees believe that the personal benefits outweigh the anxieties.

There are other ways the devotees can serve. The administration of ISKCON's affairs involves a host of secretaries, receptionists, computer specialists, financial advisers, and liaison workers. The publication and distribution of books and magazines demands a substantial technical staff. Running the day-to-day affairs of the temple requires a staff of cooks, cleaners, religious specialists, public affairs workers, and ground staff. In addition, there are the people who run the nursery, the school, the guest programmes, the training programmes, and the restaurants. In some sense all are engaged in *sankirtana*.

What the Hare Krishna way of life represents is an interesting combination of East and West. Since the late nineteenth century Indian teachers and sectarian leaders have shown a desire to take the religion and culture of the subcontinent to the 'occident'. Very often this mission has taken the form of a gift of spirituality: the East offers its religious tradition to the materially and technologically able but now spiritually bankrupt West. This view, however, has provoked sharp criticism from some Indian scholars. In reality the religion of India, they say, is not a religion of spirituality but a religion of worldliness and attention to correct behaviour and conduct. It is the West itself which has drawn a spiritual message from the East because of its own religious preconceptions. [12]

This is not the place to unravel the intricacies of this debate. It is important to remember, however, that the devotional movement popularized in the sixteenth century by Chaitanya was most certainly both spiritual and missionary in its orientation. [13] These qualities might account for some of its contemporary success in the West. Here, where religion has traditionally had an underlying, if rather élitist, preoccupation with questions about the soul, the meaning of life, our relationship with God, and the afterlife, these qualities are bound to be attractive. However, the spiritual and missionary elements of this form of devotionalism are not new. They were not added by Prabhupada to make the message more palatable to his Western disciples. Not only are the broad concepts and general practices (such as *karma, bhakti,* deity worship, and guru lineage) familiar to all Hindus, whether they live in the subcontinent or elsewhere, but the specific forms these concepts and practices take are familiar in India too. This has been shown in the case of *sankirtana,* the practice of public preaching, as well as in the practice of chanting. Both have their origins in sixteenth-century Bengal. Just as contemporary Anglicanism owes its origins to the European Renaissance and the Reformation, so the Hare Krishna movement owes its origins to a North Indian religious renaissance.

What, then, has the West contributed? Religious movements, even tight-knit monastic communities, find it almost impossible to exist in isolation from their social and geographical context. The missionary character of the Hare Krishna movement binds it firmly to its surroundings. As a consequence, its membership is local, bringing with it its particular social and cultural influences. Even those Indians who join the movement or lend it their support are part of a community which has already imbibed many of the values and traditions of Western society. Many of its social operations are determined by contemporary trends (computer technology, selling techniques, video, etc.). Members of the movement, while having a commitment to spreading an uncompromised message, nevertheless recognize the value of working within existing frameworks. The message remains pure, but it moves in mysterious ways.

4
Hare Krishna from the Outside

When the Pope came to Britain in 1982 he was the star attraction in the media for two whole weeks. More recently, the Bishop of Durham stirred up controversy with his views on the virgin birth and the resurrection. Religion on such occasions becomes newsworthy. [1] The Hare Krishna movement, along with groups like the Moonies, Scientology, and the 'orange' followers of Bhagwan Rajneesh, has a similar potential for exciting interest. It is controversial. It is colourful. It is exotic and unusual. Well-known people are attracted to it. It is largely a youth movement, and thus prone to deviate from society's expectations. What is more, it has a public profile: it is 'out there', on the streets.

It is through the filter of the media that the general public sees the Hare Krishna movement. So, what kind of image of the Hare Krishna movement have the media presented?

In 1984 the newspaper coverage dealing with the movement focused on the political and legal issues concerning 'cults' and on the famous personalities attracted to the Hare Krishna movement. In the first area the attitude was generally critical, whereas the attitude taken in the second was more generous. In 1984 the Cottrell Report was debated in the European Parliament (calling for voluntary guidelines to curb 'sects'), and Lord Denning proposed withdrawing the cults' charitable status. [2] It was also the year during which a number of leading personalities from the entertainment world took to Krishna Consciousness. In reporting the opinions of the leading characters in these stories — Richard Cottrell, Lord Denning, Hayley Mills, Hazel O'Connor and Annie Lennox — the newspaper coverage was correspondingly unfavourable or favourable in its account. [3]

Some papers are careful to describe potentially controversial issues like Hare Krishna in a straightforward and unbiased fashion: most of the serious dailies and many local newspapers usually work in this way. [4] Others approach the Hare Krishna movement, and other religious groups, with implied prejudice and resentment. Even in articles which outwardly favour the movement, the language used is belittling and reveals an underlying sense of suspicion. 'Star singer's odd passion for a guru' was how one paper described Annie Lennox's marriage to a devotee, while another member of the movement, responsible for public relations and recruitment, was entitled 'The Persuader', and her personal manner described as 'sinister'. [5]

Television, a still more powerful medium, has also managed to present the Hare Krishna movement as dangerous. One BBC report stimulated angry letters from devotees, from sympathetic Indian Hindus, and from scholars. [6] The movement had been described as a dangerous brainwashing cult, the members of which engaged in mind-dulling chanting and worship. Several years before, however, the movement had been favourably portrayed in a series of programmes about new religious groups. [7] The response to this was quite different. After the programme members of the public approached devotees in the streets or telephoned the temples to praise their work, their lifestyle, and their commitment. [8]

Turning now to parents and the police we can appreciate that the views they hold are not entirely of their own making. Underlying any interchange with devotees — regardless of whether they are sons, daughters, or law-breakers — is the commonly-held media image. In the early days of the movement fears about Hare Krishna were greater than they are now, with some justification. Many young people at that time were involved in a variety of activities which appeared strange and disturbing to their parents. Many were taking drugs. Some were dropping out of college and university, following the 'hippy trail' to the East or joining some new-fangled mystical group in a rural retreat. From the outside, all these things appeared to be part of the same package. How was a parent to know that Hare Krishna shunned 'free love' and drug taking and that it was part of an established religious tradition?

Nowadays things are different. The fears are still there, but Hare Krishna is part of a different social context, being now an established religious group rather than a new youth movement. The leaders of the movement are in their thirties and early forties, often with teenage children of their own. Some parents become so impressed with the philosophy taken up by their children that they become involved themselves. In fact, a whole range of relationships exist between devotees and their relatives, from mutual animosity to family love and attentiveness. This range of feelings was well illustrated in 1983 when a young female devotee was kidnapped by several men, commonly

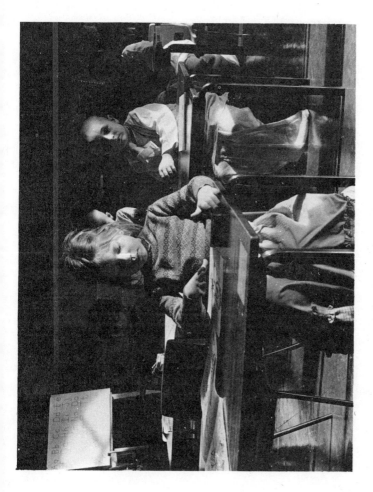

Hare Krishna children.

Hare Krishna Children.

known as 'deprogrammers' or 'faithbreakers', at her mother's arrangement. [9] According to the devotee's mother, she was doing this for her daughter's good. She believed that Hare Krishna was an evil sect, and that she was acting in the interest of her daughter in trying to remove her from its clutches. The girl's father, however, took a quite different attitude. He said that although his daughter had not had his blessings when she had joined the movement, she was obviously happy and had a right to make up her own mind.

Adverse views of the movement suggest a strong element of fear. Parents are afraid that irreparable harm will be done to their children if they remain in the movement. These fears are largely brought about by a clash of religious interests. This new religious group, like the Moonies, is seen to be intrinsically evil. The effects of this attitude have been threefold. Some parents have resorted to the kind of illegal practices described above to remove their children from the 'dangers' of the cult. Though this has only happened on one occasion to a British Hare Krishna devotee, it is more common in other European countries and in the United States. It is particularly unpleasant because it brings together the genuine, if misguided, fears of parents, and the unacceptable practices of the 'deprogrammers'. Religious opposition has also generated anti-cult organizations and a widespread spirit of challenge in the Churches.

In Britain there are two organizations that have pursued a campaign against new religious groups like Hare Krishna. Although only one of these is avowedly religious in its outlook (Deo Gloria Trust), both have contacts with religious organizations. Deo Gloria Trust works closely with the Evangelical Alliance and fights 'what it sees as religious error and abuse with evangelical teachings' [Beckford, 1983, p. 54]. FAIR (Family Action Information and Rescue), the second and better known of the two groups, is a 'parents' association'. It was started in 1976 by a Member of Parliament, Paul Rose, who was personally involved in a libel action against the Moonies and who wanted to establish the danger of the cults as a media issue. In the 1980s it has been led by several Anglican clergymen and has become increasingly concerned to combat, not only the Moonies, but other cults as well. It aims to collect information on such groups, to publicize their dangers, and to support and provide counselling aid for ex-members and parents.

The Deo Gloria Trust and FAIR comprise the organized anti-cult feeling in Britain. Both have links with Christian groups, although in the case of FAIR this link is wholly informal. The interest shown by the Churches extends beyond their involvement in organized campaigns against such cults, however. Quite naturally, the Churches are curious about new religious groups. They want to know whether or not these groups are truly 'religious'. They want to know how they should respond to the questions their parishioners will ask, how to distinguish between the different groups, and on what grounds the distinction should be made. They also want to know how 'fellowship' and 'truth' are to be equated in this matter. The members of these groups are fellow humans, but is the message they spread a true message?

In coping with these questions the Churches respond in a number of ways. The extremes are illustrated by two attitudes, one expressed in the *Catholic Herald,* the other in ISKCON's own literature. [10] In the former, advice was given to anxious parents on how to understand their children if they joined a new religious group. The help that was offered was based on a sensible awareness of the mental and emotional conditions of people who are deeply involved in religion. However, this sensitivity was unquestionably rooted in the assumption that in Britain there were 'some 70 new religious cults brainwashing young people'. [11] The message of the article was that the young people who join are blameless and innocent but the groups themselves are deviant: 'You can be sure your son or daughter joined for one or more such good reason — however much the movement, in reality, may thrive on fraud or fantasy'. Nowhere in the account did the writer distinguish between the different 'cults' and there was an underlying assumption that young people should be persuaded to leave such movements. The Hare Krishna movement was clearly included in the discussion because it was Hare Krishna devotees who appeared in the accompanying photograph with its caption, 'Fatal Lure'. This was quite different from the impression gained by a Church of England minister who spent a week living with devotees in 1977. According to his account the Hare Krishna way of life was a truly religious one, and the devotees had 'an obvious dedication to, and love of, God', apparent not only in their acts of worship but also their everyday activities. In this account, no distinction was made between the movement and its members. Such was his impression of the spiritual life of the movement that he reported, 'these devotees, like the early Christians, could "turn the world upside down" today!'.

These two quite different responses to the Hare Krishna movement are not in any way indicative of the general attitudes of either the Catholic Church or the Anglican Church in Britain. For many people the issue is not a closed one: they are neither vehemently opposed, nor wholeheartedly in favour. On the whole they are concerned to know and understand more about the phenomenon of new religious groups.

There is, however, a general lack of unbiased information available and a resultant lack of discrimination between the different movements. This was demonstrated in 1984 at the time of the Cottrell Report. This report, debated in the European Parliament in May 1984, urged for curbs on religious 'sects', which included the Moonies, Scientology, the followers of Bhagwan Rajneesh and Hare Krishna, although Richard Cottrell, the author of the report, inferred that there were many more. Although the report did not call for formal legislation, it did ask for voluntary guidelines to keep the sects in check, ranging from innocuous requests, such as members being allowed to continue education courses on joining, to proposals for requiring groups to make their membership lists publicly available. [12]

It was not so much the content of the report that was alarming to many people as its implications. The particular target, according to the author, was the Moonies; but as many religious organizations were quick to point out — not just the other new religious groups themselves, but the ethnic minority religions and the established Christian denominations — its effects could be more widespread. Religious freedom, indeed civil liberty as a whole, it was argued, would suffer as a consequence of this motion being passed.

Although some religious representatives were genuinely concerned about the rights of the sects and their members, many more were worried about the damage that might be done to their own religious freedom if such a motion were to be widely accepted throughout Europe. This fear was revitalized later in the same year when Lord Denning called for an inquiry in the House of Lords into religious cults. He was particularly worried about what he saw as the abuse of their charitable status. He sought a High Court Declaration to affirm that the cults were not religious and thus not qualified to be registered as charities. In conjunction with this he wanted to see all religious groups licensed by a Commissioner of Religious Bodies. The danger in which all religions would find themselves, whether they were cults, sects, or established denominations, was quite clear from this: the idea of an 'independent' assessor making decisions on what might or might not count as religion was an intolerable threat to personal and organizational freedom. As a result of this, some established Church bodies supported the new religions, albeit implicitly, against such attempts to infringe their rights. [13]

As Lord Denning himself pointed out, the problem for those who feared cult practices was that young people over the age of eighteen could not be hindered from joining cults if they chose to do so. It was a straightforward question of freedom of choice. At that age a person became free to make all kinds of decisions about their lifestyle and future, including their religious identity.

The same desire to protect freedom and guard against those who abuse it motivates the police in their dealings with new religious groups. The Hare Krishna movement, more than any of the other new religious movements, has a high profile with the police. [14] Its chanting party is constantly out on the streets in London, and from time to time, in other British towns and cities, and its members are frequently to be found in shopping areas distributing books and food, and asking for donations. They also sell paintings or sets of books door-to-door. Every Sunday large numbers of people visit Bhaktivedanta Manor, causing potential problems for other road users. The police understandably take an interest in these activities, not because of the Hare Krishna involvement but because these are activities in which the law can be broken or the rights of others can be abused.

This is not a straightforward issue. The law never is. What, for example, constitutes 'obstruction'? How are the rights of residents to be balanced with the right which people have to visit their place of worship? It is a part of the religious duty of devotees to chant in the streets, to bring the holy name (*harinama*) to the attention of the public. In their efforts to teach people about Krishna and Krishna Consciousness the devotees give away enormous quantities of food and literature. As they see it, asking people to support their charitable efforts seems justified. People can always say 'No'. However, many devotees would probably admit that the temptation to say that the collection of money is for some general charitable cause rather than for the movement itself is very great, because the public has been given such a bad impression of Hare Krishna. For the less experienced devotees it is sometimes hard to be honest under such circumstances. [15]

In the past, cases brought to court by the police nearly always resulted in a win by the prosecution: devotees simply accepted the situation and pleaded guilty. Today the movement makes greater efforts to understand the law, operate within it, and defend cases that are brought to court. For example, efforts have been made by the movement to abide by the guidelines relating to street activity and obstruction. As a result, fewer charges have been made, and there have been fewer prosecutions.

Despite inevitable confrontations, relations between the Hare Krishna movement and the British police are good. New officers at the Hendon Police Training School now visit Bhaktivedanta Manor to meet devotees as part of their initial training.

What this shows is that at the local level efforts are made by both sides to maintain good relations. For the police, for parents and relatives, for Church representatives, even for the media, relations with the movement are generally good where there is close contact. Parents

Devotees petitioning at Downing Street.

whose children have been involved in the movement for some years, and who have taken the trouble to visit Bhaktivedanta Manor and meet the other devotees, usually come away feeling reassured. Members of the clergy who have met and talked to Hare Krishna leaders at inter-faith meetings, or by invitation at ISKCON centres, are generally appreciative of the spiritual and practical commitment of the devotees. The local press tends to be less sensationalist and emotive in its accounts of Hare Krishna than at a national level.

For those who have come into more direct contact with the movement — parents, clergy, press and police alike — the devotees have become real people. From being eccentric and exotically-clad social dropouts with unaccountable habits and interests they have become fellow humans living a genuinely religious life.

5

The Hare Krishna Movement
in Perspective

Despite the fact that the Hare Krishna devotees look so different from
the rest of us and engage in activities which to most of us would be
unpalatable, they are still part of a world which we know and
understand. We are all in the same world, in the same space and time.
The difference is that we do not interpret this world in the same way.
The explanation we give to things is not the same as the devotees'. Life
and death have a different meaning for them, and their way of life,
like ours, is organized to suit this meaning. The devotees have not
always believed as they do or lived as they do now though. For
most of them these beliefs and practices belong only to their adult
lives. They were converted to them. They can remember a time
when they were us — when they were shopping in Oxford Street,
not chanting there.

Those who have joined the Hare Krishna movement, and remain
in it either as full-time devotees or congregational members, have
decided that here is a religion which can help them answer their
questions about human life and purpose in a way other religious and
social groups have been unable to do. New questions naturally arise,
and life continues to be hard; but the devotees know *why* it is hard
and how best to cope with it.

Put this way, the space between those inside the movement and
those outside diminishes. What at times can seem like an
insurmountable barrier betwen 'us and them' becomes nothing more
than the simple and inevitable differences between people of any sort.

Looking beneath the surface of the movement has shown us three
things. Hare Krishna is not a new religious group, except in the most
superficial sense; it is not stuck in the cultural and social groove of the
1960s; nor is it just one of many contemporary cults, and hence
interchangeable with Divine Light, the Moonies, or the Rajneesh
movement. None of these stereotypes do justice to the Hare Krishna

devotees, their philosophy, and their way of life. Their religion is firmly rooted in Indian tradition. It is dynamic. It has characteristics which distinguish it from other contemporary religious groups and which qualify it to stand independently as a 'bona fide' religion. [1]

These conclusions are worth emphasizing in detail. Though Krishna Consciousness was new to Britain in the late 1960s and early 1970s it had well-established links with the devotional movement of sixteenth-century Bengal, and through that with earlier theistic Hinduism. In addition, most of its 'lay' followers, the Indian Hindu membership, regard it as a genuine expression of *Krishna bhakti*.

Krishna Consciousness, according to the devotees, is best fostered by a return to *Vedic* principles and practices. [2] The spiritual discipline and asceticism of chanting, early rising, abstention from meat, intoxicants, illicit sex, and gambling is an important part of this. In addition, general cultural behaviour — dress, diet, educational and social values — is informed by it. To the devotees the past is 'vital' in two senses: it is important, and it is alive in the present.

For the devotees Krishna Consciousness represents the knowledge of *Vedic* literature passed down through the chain of disciplic succession. [3] It is the message of devotion to God (*bhakti*) revealed in the *Bhagavad Gita*, as well as the method of congregational chanting and preaching (*sankirtana*) practised by Chaitanya Mahaprabhu. Scholars of religion, too, have begun to examine the relationship between the Hare Krishna movement in the West and the tradition of *bhakti* Hinduism in India. [4]

The Hare Krishna movement, then, is formally related to a tradition of considerable historical stature in India. [5] Like all groups which advocate a return to a Golden Age, however, Krishna Consciousness represents the past suspended in the present. It stresses the lifestyle and values of another time, but the practice of living this lifestyle and of living according to these values is contingent upon the particular demands of the present. The 'here and now' is itself not static. The political, economic, and legal system in which devotees find themselves, the contemporary social and psychological conditions, as well as the geographical context, are all slowly changing. Living in a religious community and spreading a religious message are influenced by this changing context. We have seen how the law determines the nature of preaching activity, and how contemporary social arrangements, and the values associated with them, have an impact on styles of membership and internal relationships. The movement has also adapted itself to geographical, political, and economic conditions in other countries. Life for devotees in North America, for instance, is very different to life for those in African

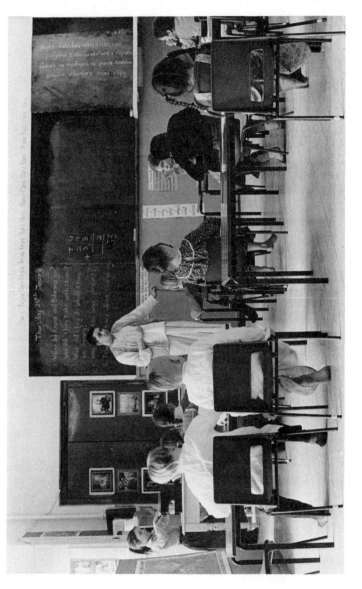

The Krishna Consciousness Gurukula (School).

countries, or Italy, or Japan, or in the Communist bloc. Many of the same practices of course pertain. Devotees everywhere participate in the morning programme of worship, chanting, learning, and food sharing. They also perform some kind of *sankirtana* or preaching. What kind, however, will depend upon the location. In the USSR, *sankirtana* will be conducted in a very different way from in Europe. But when *sankirtana* can mean anything from a public lecture to a conversation, from the sale of expensive paintings to the gift of a small book, from the invitation to a formal feast to the sharing of simple food, the scope is immense. The message, however, remains the same.

This has also been true for the movement in Britain since its arrival here in 1969. At first the way of life and the ways of spreading the message were simple. Money was in short supply, living conditions were fairly basic, and the devotees' service was largely limited to public chanting and distribution. Since then many changes have taken place. The way of life, though perhaps austere by our normal standards and expectations, is comfortable and the emphasis is now more squarely placed on Krishna Consciousness 'at home', on devotion to God through ordinary family life. Hare Krishna is not just a life of dancing in Oxford Street, and a collection of old hippies trapped in a 1960s mentality. A more reliable image might now be the Sunday programme at Bhaktivedanta Manor at which full-time members and local FOLK devotees are present and where, over the course of the day, the predominant group is the Indian Hindu community, large numbers of which now chant at home, read the movement's books, visit the temple regularly and attend classes given by the guru.

Rooted in tradition, Hare Krishna is thus an adaptable movement, capable of adjusting itself to specific local conditions. By presenting a consistent message in new and different ways it has continued to attract a small but steadily growing interest from all sections of society. Krishna Consciousness is not just for those who want to live a monastic life. It is a congregational religion. Although devotees see it as essential to retain a group of fully-committed specialists able not only to conduct worship but also to exemplify a life of regulation and service, they also recognize that the future lies 'out there'. As they see it, Krishna Consciousness is for everyone, not just for a monastic élite; consequently it is their duty to see that it is made available to everyone.

Because the Hare Krishna movement is part of the well-established, Indian *Vaishnava* tradition, and because it presents the principles and practices of *Vaishnavism* in new and changing contexts, it follows that it is not simply a youth movement offering nothing more than a meditation technique and a new set of clothes. It offers a complete religious way of life rather than a set of techniques. This is not to suggest

Bhagavandas Goswami with children.

that other movements labelled with the word 'new' offer no more than techniques for a peaceful experience or the reduction of stress. Some of them do present themselves in this way; but others, like Hare Krishna, offer more complex practices and beliefs. In addition a number of groups, regardless of the level of commitment they require or the nature of their objectives, have their roots in established religious traditions. To push all these groups together as if they were philosophically, practically, or culturally interchangeable is misleading. Yet to resist this is not to negate the value of examining the rise and proliferation of 'new religious movements' in general. By taking this 'horizontal' approach, it is possible to consider such sociological questions as 'Who joins these groups?', 'Why do people join?', and 'How do these groups as a whole relate to other social and religious institutions in contemporary society?'. Such questions have been addressed by a number of scholars in recent years. [6]

Nevertheless, the 'horizontal' approach, which views new religious groups as a single social phenomenon, has a potential for distortion. For those who are not predisposed to be favourable towards such groups the question of who joins is not just concerned with social backgrounds: it becomes part of a wider questioning about the power of leadership and the gullibility of new members. What starts as an objective, sociological question about membership can become a subjective crusade against 'brainwashing' and 'coercion'. It is perfectly possible to discuss new religious groups as a single social phenomenon without making offensive and inaccurate generalizations. It is important to remember, however, that this phenomenon is composed of a number of quite separate religious organizations, each deserving detailed, independent analysis. This view, which might be described as the 'vertical' approach to understanding new religious movements, encourages us to see each group not just as part of a general social and cultural climate peculiar to a fixed historical period, but as a separate movement with specific beliefs and practices and an independent history. [7] Using this approach the questions we should ask relate to a specific group rather than to new religious movements as a whole. 'What are its origins?' 'What do its adherents believe and practise?' 'What attracted people to this group?' 'How has it changed?'

These questions apply equally to all those groups referred to as 'new' regardless of the antiquity of their origins. To a group like Hare Krishna questions relating to historical change are clearly of great significance. However, even those groups which are obviously new have developed and changed since their inception in the 1960s and 1970s. What will happen to such movements in the future? Will they become part of the established religious scene? Will people begin to see them as genuine religious sects rather than new-fangled youth cults? For the Hare Krishna movement at least some kind of future seems assured. It has a sound international framework with centres in over fifty countries and publications in as many languages. It has a Governing Body Commission to deal with international management, and a body of *gurus* and *sannyasis* to provide spiritual leadership. It has a monastic system and a broad-based and increasingly effective congregational network. All this is contained within a timeless philosophy and a way of life which expresses this philosophy. As the devotees see it, it is the quality of the message, combined with the disenchantment brought on by modern society, which makes ISKCON work. And yet despite the missionary enthusiasm and commitment of the devotees, most people in Britain, whether committed or nominal in their allegiance, continue to see themselves as Christians. [8] Hare Krishna continues, numerically, to be a small religious movement. The media attention it receives and its high profile on our streets perhaps lead us to believe it to be larger than it is. But its size has nothing to do with its cultural and social significance. With its emphasis on serving God, and on self-realization within a life of dedication and commitment, Krishna Consciousness is an authentic religious option.

Notes

Introduction

1   This point is made in an article on conversion, brainwashing and deprogramming (Richardson, 1982, p. 49).
2   See Richardson (1982, p. 44).
3   This figure of 9,000 is an amalgamation of those on the Bhaktivedanta Book Trust mailing list and those who have taken out life membership to ISKCON. For more information, see Chapter Two.
4   A brief history of the movement is provided in Chapter One.
5   This phrase was often used by Prabhupada to describe his mission in the West. It is a translation of Chaitanya Mahaprabhu's own plea for the spread of his system of *Krishna bhakti* (Prabhupada, *Sri Caitanya-caritamrta*, Antya-lila, Chapter One, p. 59).

Chapter One

1   Members of the Hare Krishna movement are generally referred to as 'devotees'.
2   The different social divisions within the movement are described in more detail in Chapter Two.
3   The hair and the other distinguishing features are discussed in an introductory pamphlet produced by the movement, *An Introduction to Krishna Consciousness* (ISKCON, n.d.).
4   They are, in fact, *Vaishnava* marks associated with the worship of the God Vishnu and the other deities to which he is related, including Krishna and Rama.
5   These are all names for Indian religious leaders. See Glossary.
6   The Hindu religious tradition, its beliefs and practices are examined in *Hinduism* (Zaehner, 1962), *The Hindu Religious Tradition* (Hopkins, 1971) and *The Sacred Thread* (Brockington, 1981).
7   For a discussion of the nature of Krishna see *KRSNA, The Supreme Personality of Godhead* (Prabhupada, 1970), and *Srimad Bhagavatam* Cantos 1-10 (Prabhupada, 1972-80).

8   Groups like Transcendental Meditation, the followers of Meher Baba, the Divine Light Mission, Ananda Marga Yoga, and Raja Yoga were all established in the West during these decades. Some of the general principles of Indian philosophy and lifestyle were apparent in more ordinary situations, however. Extra-mural yoga classes sprang up everywhere. Many people became more concerned about diet, some taking to vegetarianism. Even meditation became a common phenomenon.

9   This philosophical stance is referred to as 'non-dualism' or *advaita vedanta*. It will be referred to further later in this chapter.

10   For more information on Hindu deities, see *Hindu Myths* (O'Flaherty, 1975).

11   For further reading on Chaitanya Mahaprabhu, see *Sri Caitanya-caritamrta* (Prabhupada, 1974-5) and the short biographical accounts in Judah (1974), Mangalvadi (1977), Eck (1979), and Gelberg (1983).

12   Useful introductory materials on the Indian philosophers are *The Essentials of Indian Philosophy* (Hiriyanna, 1949) and *Hindu Patterns of Liberation* (Open University, 1978).

13   The philosophical approach articulated by Shankara — *advaita vedanta* — provides the precedent for many twentieth-century groups and religious leaders. The popularity of what has now become commonly and misleading known as *vedanta* was mentioned earlier in this chapter and may be seen in the works of Ramakrishna and Vivekananda, the *Theosophical Society,* Christopher Isherwood, Maharishi Mahesh Yogi (*TM*), and Krishnamurti.

14   The system of guru lineage or disciplic succession (*parampara*) is the route by which all Indian schools of philosophy pass on and authenticate their teachings.

15   A six-volume account of the life of A. C. Bhaktivedanta Swami Prabhupada has been compiled by Satsvarupa dasa Goswami, *Srila Prabhupada-lilamrta* (1980-3). A shortened version of the biography is also available (Goswami, 1983[b]).

16   These early disciples are introduced in volume two of *Srila Prabhupada-lilamrta,* 'Planting the Seed, 1965-6' (Goswami, 1980[a]).

17   The name given to the general devotional practices initiated by Chaitanya Mahaprabhu is *sankirtana.* This term refers to all kinds of preaching and missionary activity, to distributing books and food, to talking about Krishna Consciousness to others, and particularly to chanting the holy name in public. *Kirtana* is the specific name given to this last activity, to singing and dancing with Krishna in mind.

18   These were two religious movements founded in the late nineteenth century in India with a mission in the West.

19   George Harrison talks about his encounters with the devotees in *Chant and Be Happy* (ISKCON, 1982), and in *Srila Prabhupada lilamrta* vol. 4 (Goswami, 1982).

20   Each year a procession of chariots is held called the *Rathayatra* festival

(after its equivalent in Pure in the Indian State of Orissa). The deities known as Jagannatha, Baladeva and Subhadra are drawn through the streets on large carts.

21 The *Daily Mirror* printed a favourable article on the school with a large picture of the Hare Krishna children sitting on the floor in the temple: 'It's just 4.30 a.m. . . . but classes have begun at Britain's most amazing school' (28 January 1984, p. 3).

22 These three initiatives are discussed in Chapter Two.

23 The regulative principles — strict vegetarianism, no intoxicants, no illicit sex, and no gambling — are described in some detail in the second half of Chapter Three.

24 In Chapter Two initiation figures are presented which illustrate the disruption within the movement during recent years.

25 The question of the role of the guru in relation to the spiritual lineage and ISKCON's Governing Body Commission is discussed by Larry Shinn and Steven Gelberg in *Hare Krishna, Hare Krishna* (Gelberg, 1983, pp. 77-84). They discuss the responsibility of a guru to his disciples, the relationship of the guru to the rest of the Krishna Consciousness movement, and the ramifications of the fall of a guru.

26 George Harrison's close relationship with Krishna Consciousness was affirmed in a second popular record 'My Sweet Lord' in 1970. He talks about the meaning of this song in *Chant and Be Happy . . . The Story of the Hare Krishna Mantra* (ISKCON, 1982, pp. 31-33).

Chapter Two

1 Thomas Luckmann suggested a variety of popular, non-religious themes which provide meaning for people today in *The Invisible Religion* (1967).

2 The 'counter-culture' has been discussed in many recent accounts of contemporary religion and society. One of the earliest and most useful of these is *Making of a Counter Culture* (Roszak, 1970). The study which does most justice to the Hare Krishna movement in these early years is *Hare Krishna and the Counterculture* (Judah, 1974).

3 There are also at the time of writing about fifty full-time devotees in Eire.

4 Initiation is discussed in some detail in Chapter Three.

5 Those who joined in 1983 were initiated in 1984, making this figure the most up-to-date available at the time of writing.

6 These figures represent only those initiated devotees who had undertaken the introductory course. In 1984 there were in fact 61 initiations. Four people had reached this stage of commitment and maturity without taking part in a formal training programme.

7 A number of scholars speculated on the future of the movement. Their conclusions were generally pessimistic (Mangalvadi, 1977; Johnson, 1976). Francine Daner was slightly more cautious in her analysis (1976).

8 The content of the initiation ceremony will be discussed in Chapter Three.

9 The current guru for Britain, Bhagavandas Goswami, is constantly being

asked questions about the paths of women devotees. At a festival in August 1984 he said there was no reason why women should not be heads of department within ISKCON, or temple presidents. On another occasion he was asked whether a woman could become a renunciate or even a guru. He replied that 'Sannyasa is ultimately a renounced mentality whereby one understands, "Everything belongs to Krsna and nothing is mine; therefore what do I have to renounce?" Anyone who is firmly situated in this consciousness is qualified to be a guru and engage you in devotional service' (ISKCON, *Gurudevamrta*, 2: 34, 1984, p. 20).

10   Several newspaper articles informed readers of the spiritual interests of Hayley Mills, Hazel O'Connor, and Annie Lennox of 'Eurhythmics' (e.g. *Daily Mail*, 19 June 1984; *The London Standard*, 23 August 1984; *Cosmopolitan*, October 1984).

11   In a Gallup survey, 30 per cent of people between the ages of 18 and 30 said they believed in reincarnation. On the subject of vegetarianism, the movement has not only produced vegetarian cookery books, held evening classes and distributed vegetarian food in conjunction with its programmes of work and worship, it has also fed large numbers of people at its restaurant in Central London. (Another has been opened in Leicester).

12   The relationship of the Indian Hindu community in Britain to the Hare Krishna movement was made the subject of a recent empirical study by Sean Carey (1983).

13   In recent years a body of literature has developed which discusses the migration and settlement of Indian Hindus in East Africa and Britain. The East African period is examined particularly by Morris (1968) and Bharati (1972); the British settlement is discussed in Bowen (1981), Knott (1981, 1982), and Michaelson (1983). Academic interest continues to be shown in this area as was illustrated by a seminar series held in 1985 at the School of Oriental and African Studies in London on the theme of 'Hinduism in Britain'. The papers presented in this series are to be published and will include a contribution on the Hare Krishna movement, in addition to papers on particular Hindu communities in Britain and other related themes.

14   For most ordinary people, regardless of their ethnic extraction, the austerity demanded by this way of life is unattractive. However, just because most Hindus do not choose to live like this does not stop them from feeling that perhaps they should try harder to lead a more spiritual life. Some believe that Britain has exposed them to new pressures, opportunities, and temptations which make this difficult. Life in the subcontinent of India, however, although more informed by ritual practice and the Hindu social system, was no more 'spiritual' than life here. The West has brought more distractions but for various reasons it has also brought a greater 'awareness' of the concerns of spirituality. Hinduism is certainly a tradition in which spiritual questions, paths, and goals play a part; but most Hindus — like most people everywhere

— are driven by more pragmatic concerns. The Hare Krishna movement has brought to the attention of Hindus in this country the spiritual aspects of the tradition of which they are a part.

15 The stories attached to these historical developments can be read in *Srila Prabhupada-lilamrta*, vol. 4, ch. 2 (1982).

16 The parking problems experienced during this festival are notorious, and relations with local residents are at times strained as a result.

17 According to Carey (1983), 35 of the 400 full-time devotees in Britain in the early 1980s were Indians.

18 This was the title given to a national meeting held in Leicester in December 1984 at which the future of Hinduism in Britain was discussed by temple representatives, other Hindu leaders, Members of Parliament, and the ethnic press.

Chapter Three

1 For an explanation of these terms, see Glossary.

2 For details of the disciplic lineage of the Krishna Consciousness movement see Prabhupada (1972, p. 28).

3 When Krishna appears in the form of an *avatara* (incarnation) He is still unlimited. He is not qualified by the form in which He manifests Himself. He appears to be like us but is not actually like us.

4 Prabhupada was renowned for his use of analogies. This one appears in *The Nectar of Devotion* (Prabhupada, 1970[a], p. xviii).

5 This is discussed in *The Science of Self-Realisation*, Section Two (Prabhupada, 1977).

6 All devotees take the additional title *dasa* or *dasi*, meaning 'servant'.

7 Perhaps this is why so much of Prabhupada's personal vocabulary (e.g. words and phrases such as 'part and parcel', 'ecstatic', 'spirit souls' and 'association') is adopted by the devotees.

8 The case of Jayatirtha dasa (see Chapter One) illustrates this.

9 Those just setting out on the path of Krishna Consciousness — the *bhaktas* and *bhaktins* on the introductory course — are expected to be more rigorous in their self-education. They attend additional daytime classes and read set passages from the scriptures as part of their training.

10 The *Mangalarti* prayers, which are sung, concern three characters understood to be 'dear to the heart of Krishna': the spiritual master or guru, without whom Krishna's mercy cannot be obtained; Nrsimha Deva, the incarnation of Krishna who is half-man and half-lion in form, and is held to be the supreme protector and refuge; Tulsi Devi, who is worshipped in the form of the tulsi plant, and who helps to fulfil the wishes of the devotees of Krishna.

11 The second of the daily services begins with a song in praise of the beauty of Krishna. This is followed by obeisances in verse form to Prabhupada and the current spiritual master for this area, Srila Gurudeva. While these are sung the devotees offer flowers to the feet of the image of their spiritual master. One disciple will then lead the others in singing the Hare Krishna mantra.

12   Several scholars have been of this opinion although the only account which is easily available is Chaudhuri (1980).

13   This is supported by the independent scholars interviewed in a recent book on the Hare Krishna movement (Gelberg, 1983).

Chapter Four

1   I have written about the relationship between religion and the media elsewhere after working for eighteen months on a research project which investigated this question (Knott, 1984).

2   These proposals are discussed in more detail later in this chapter.

3   For examples see 'Moves to check religious sects', Bristol *Evening Post*, 22 May 1984; 'Denning calls for enquiry into religious cults', *Daily Telegraph*, 12 July 1984; 'Hayley's just wild about Hare . . . and her man', *Daily Mail*, 19 June 1984; 'Hazel breaks new ground', *The London Standard*, 23 August 1984; 'Annie gets her hun', *Cosmopolitan*, October 1984.

4   The *Guardian* and, on occasions, *The Times* portray the movement in a somewhat more serious manner (e.g. 'Member kidnapped says sect', the *Guardian*, 9 February 1983, 'Hare Krishnas add a touch of colour to Capability Brown', *The Times*, 27 June 1984). *The London Standard* frequently prints favourable articles, as do the Hertfordshire newspapers which serve the area in which the majority of full-time devotees live (e.g. *Herts Advertiser, Post* (Borehamwood, Elstree, Radlett, Edgware), *Herts and Essex Observer, Watford Observer*, and *Hitchen Gazette*).

5   The most serious case of this occurred in August 1984 when two brothers were arrested for murder at the Soho Street temple after a tip-off to police by the movement. The men had tried to join the movement at Bhaktivedanta Manor, and devotees had later become suspicious and informed the police. Some of the national newspaper headlines, however, despite heading articles which made this situation clear, suggested a more intimate connection between the movement and the crimes committed by these men. One paper began its short article with 'Krishna arrests' while another entitled its contribution 'Temple raided in deaths hunt'. Although neither headline is actually incorrect, both imply that Hare Krishna devotees were themselves under suspicion rather than helping the police to catch two dangerous criminals.

6   This report was presented in BBC 1's 'Nationwide', 14 March 1983.

7   This programme (7 June 1981) was part of the 'Credo' series, made by London Weekend Television for ITV.

8   An account is given of the response received after the 'Credo' programme in *FOLK Magazine*, Summer 1981.

9   This case was reported in the national press (e.g. *The London Standard*, 9 February 1983; *Daily Mirror*, 9 February 1983; the *Guardian*, 9 February 1983).

10   These responses appeared in the *Catholic Herald*, 28 September 1984 (Coping with religious cults', p. 5) and *Who Are They?*, ISKCON,

1982[a] ('Inter-Faith Dialogue', p. 27).

11   The concept of 'brainwashing', and the question of whether it occurs in new religious movements is discussed in Bromley and Shupe (1981), Richardson (1982), and Barker (1984).

12   A report of Richard Cottrell's motion to the European Parliament was printed in the Bristol *Evening Post*, 22 May 1984.

13   Lord Dennings' call in the House of Lords for an enquiry into the cults issue, and some of the subsequent letters of response were printed in the *Daily Telegraph* in the summer of 1984.

14   In Britain the devotees have made much effort to improve relations with both the police and the Charity Commissioners in order to avoid unnecessary problems. Public Affairs and Legal Departments have been set up for this purpose.

15   One of the initiatives which has made the business of street collecting easier for everyone concerned — devotees, police, and public alike — is the attempt leaders have made to fully legalize this activity. Previously devotees would collect in streets, at doors and in shopping centres regardless of the local restrictions placed on such behaviour. Nowadays ISKCON, like other registered charities, places formal applications with local councils for the allocation of specific 'collection days' in their areas. The process of collecting money from the public is now fully legalized.

Chapter Five

1   ISKCON was declared to be a 'bona fide' religious group by a New York High Court Justice in March 1977 who threw out two charges against the leaders of the movement of 'illegal imprisonment' and 'attempted extortion'. This occasion was seen by the movement as recognition of their authentic religious status, particularly as their case had been supported by the American Union for Civil Liberties and various established religious organizations (Goswami, 1983[a], p. 267).

2   Looking back to the *Vedic* past is inevitably a process of reinterpretation. The contemporary *Vedic* way of life is the product of a series of layers of interpretation from Chaitanya and his followers in the sixteenth century to Prabhupada and his disciples in the last two decades. What today's devotees see as *Vedic*, and how they put it into practice, will be quite different from the equivalent perspective and orientation of their sixteenth-century Bengali predecessors as a result of the geographical, historical, and social conditions pertaining in each case. Not that this makes the current attempt to return to the *Vedic* past any less worthy or worthwhile than former attempts. It is, however, important to remember what these conditions are, and to consider what impact they have in forming the way of life of devotees in the West.

3   '*Vedic* literature' is a category which includes texts according to their content not their historical age. That is to say, whereas the term 'Vedic' generally applies to the four *Vedas* up to and including the *Upanishads,* in this sense it applies to all authorized teachings which preach the

message of *Krishna bhakti* (i.e. those composed within the disciplic succession).

4 Examples of this interest are Judah (1974), Eck (1979), Klostermaier (1980), and Hopkins, Basham and Srivatsa Goswami in Gelberg (1983).

5 This is not true of all the new religious movements related to Hinduism. Some groups were founded by Indians and make use of various aspects of Hindu belief and behaviour, but are not linked to traditional philosophical schools in the way that Krishna Consciousness is (e.g. Raja Yoga, the Rajneesh movement, Divine Light Mission). Transcendental Meditation (TM) is another example of a group in which the founder is related by means of disciplic succcession to formal texts and teachings (*parampara*), although the Maharishi Mahesh Yogi has placed less emphasis than Bhaktivedanta Swami Prabhupada on an accurate historical rendition of these texts and teachings.

6 A number of scholars in the last decade have considered the sociological impact of these new movements. These include Glock and Bellah (1976), Wuthnow (1976), Wilson (1981), Bromley and Shupe (1981), Barker (1982), Wallis (1984). These studies range from collections of essays containing discussions both of individual groups and the phenomenon of new religious movements as a whole (e.g. Wilson and Barker), to general considerations of the contemporary 'new' religious scene. Wuthnow, for example, examined the new religious consciousness of the American West Coast, Bay Area. Bromley and Shupe discussed new groups in relation to their unpopular image and showed that the phenomenon was not to be feared. Wallis, with the use of ideal types, analysed the social and philosophical approach new groups take to the world around them.

7 Many studies of this type have been undertaken. Two which are strikingly different in type but are equally informative and compelling to read are Damrell (1977), a study of a *Vedanta* organization in the United States, and Barker (1984), a recent study of the Unification Church.

8 They are 'Christian' in the sense that they would say they were either 'Church of England', 'Catholic', 'Methodist', etc. if asked to state their religion on a form. In a recent, large-scale survey of religion in Leeds 81 per cent of those interviewed fell into this category (Krarup, 1983, p. 37).

Select Bibliography

Annett, Stephen, 1976, *The Many Ways of Being*, London, Abacus.

Back to Godhead, Philadelphia/Los Angeles, Bhaktivedanta Book Trust.

Barker, Eileen (ed.), 1982, *New Religious Movements: A Perspective for Understanding Society*, New York, Edwin Mellen Press.

——, 1984, *The Making of a Moonie: Brainwashing or Choice?*, Oxford, Basil Blackwell.

Beckford, James A., 1983, 'The public response to new religious movements in Britain', *Social Compass*, 30: 1, 49-62.

Bharati, Aghenananda, 1972, *The Asians in East Africa*, Chicago, Nelson-Hall.

Bowen, David (ed.), 1981, *Hinduism in England*, Bradford, Bradford College.

Brockington, J. L., 1981, *The Sacred Thread: Hinduism in its Continuity and Diversity*, Edinburgh, University of Edinburgh Press.

Bromley, David G., and Shupe, Anson D., 1981, *Strange Gods: The Great American Cult Scare*, Boston, Beacon Press.

Carey, Sean, 1983, 'The Hare Krishna Movement and Hindus in Britain', *New Community*, 10: 3, 477-86.

Chaudhuri, Nirad C., 1979, *Hinduism: A Religion to Live By*, Oxford, Oxford University Press.

Cox, Harvey, 1977, *Turning East: Americans Look to the Orient for Spirituality*, New York, Simon and Schuster.

Crowley, R. T., 1977, 'Krishna Consciousness in the West', *Update*, 1:3-4, 34-43.

Damrell, J. D., *Seeking Spiritual Meaning: The World of Vedanta*, London, Sage.

Daner, Francine, 1976, *The American Children of Krishna*, New York, Holt, Rhinehart and Winston.

Esk, Diana, 1979, 'Krishna Consciousness in historical perspective', *Back to Godhead*, 14: 10, 26-9.

Folk Magazine, London, Bhaktivedanta Book Trust.

Gelberg, Steven J. (ed.), 1983, *Hare Krishna, Hare Krishna*, New York, Grove Press.

Glock, C. Y., and Bellah, R. N. (eds.), 1976, *The New Religious Consciousness*, Berkeley, University of California Press.

Goswami, Satsvarupa dasa, 1980-3, *Srila Prabhupada-lilamrta*, 6 vols., Los Angeles, Bhaktivedanta Book Trust:

1980   1   A lifetime in preparation: India 1896-1965
1980[a]   2   Planting the seed: New York City 1965-6
1981   3   Only he could lead them: San Francisco/India 1967
1982   4   In every town and village: Around the world 1968-71
1983   5   Let there be a temple 1971-5
1983[a]   6   Uniting two worlds 1975-7.

——, 1983[b], *Prabhupada*, Los Angeles, Bhaktivedanta Book Trust.
Gurudevamrta, London, Bhaktivedanta Book Trust.
Hiriyanna, M., 1949, *The Essentials of Indian Philosophy*, London, George Allen and Unwin. (Reprint, 1978, Unwin Paperbacks.)
Hopkins, Thomas J., 1971, *The Hindu Religious Tradition*, Encino, California, Dickenson.
ISKCON, n.d., *An Introduction to Krishna Consciousness*, Bhaktivedanta Book Trust, London.
——, 1982, *Chant and Be Happy . . . The Story of the Hare Krishna Mantra*, Los Angeles, Bhaktivedanta Book Trust.
——, 1982[a], *Who Are They?*, Los Angeles, Bhaktivedanta Book Trust.
——, see *Back To Godhead*.
ISKCON (UK), *Folk Magazine; Gurudevamrta; Mahabharat Times*.
Johnson, Gregory, 1976, 'The Hare Krishna in San Francisco', in *The New Religious Consciousness*. ed. C. Y. Glock and R. N. Bellah, Berkeley, University of California Press.
Judah, J. Stillson, 1974, *Hare Krishna and the Counter Culture*, New York, Wiley.
Krarup, Helen, 1983, ' "Conventional religion and common religion in Leeds" Interview Schedule: Basic Frequencies', *Religious Research Paper 12*, unpublished paper, Department of Sociology, University of Leeds.
Klostermaier, K., 1980, 'Will India's past be American's future? Reflections on the Chaitanya Movement and its potential', *Journal of Asian and African Studies*, 15: 1-2, 94-103.
Knott, Kim, 1981, 'Hinduism in England: The Hindu population in Leeds', *Religious Research Paper 4*, unpublished paper, Department of Sociology, University of Leeds.
——, 1982, 'Hinduism in Leeds: a study of religious practice in the Indian Hindu community and in Hindu-related groups', unpublished Ph.D. thesis, University of Leeds.
——, 1984, 'Sorcery, Scientology, swamis and sea monsters: researchers say religion is still big news in the media', *Religion Today*, 1: 2-3, 3-5.
Luckmann, Thomas, 1967, *The Invisible Religion*, London, Collier-Macmillan.
Mahabharat Times, Watford, ISKCON Press.
Mangalvadi, Vishal, 1977, *The World of the Gurus*, Delhi, Vikas.
Michaelson, Maureen, 1983, 'Caste, kinship and marriage: a study of two

Gujarati trading castes in England', unpublished Ph.D. thesis, University of London, School of Oriental and African Studies.

Morris, H. S., 1968, *The Indians in Uganda,* Chicago, University of Chicago Press.

Needleman, Jacob, 1972, *The New Religions,* London, Allen Lane.

O'Flaherty, Wendy D., 1975, *Hindu Myths,* Harmondsworth, Penguin.

Open Univeristy, 1978, *Hindu Patterns of Liberation* (Man's Religious Quest [AD 208], Units 6-8), Milton Keynes, The Open University Press.

Prabhupada, A. C. Bhaktivedanta Swami, 1970, *Krsna: The Supreme Personality of Godhead,* New York, Bhaktivedanta Book Trust.

——, 1970[a], *The Nectar of Devotion: The Complete Science of Bhakti Yoga,* New York, Bhaktivedanta Book Trust.

——, 1972, *Bhagavad-gita As It Is,* London, Collier-Macmillan.

——, 1972[a], *The Perfection of Yoga,* New York, Bhaktivedanta Book Trust.

——, 1972-80, *Srimad Bhagavatam,* Cantos 1-10, 30 vols., New York/Los Angeles, Bhaktivedanta Book Trust.

——, 1973, *Raja-vidya: The King of Knowledge,* New York, Bhaktivedanta Book Trust.

——, 1974-5, *Sri Caitanya-caritamrta,* 17 vols., Los Angeles, Bhaktivedanta Book Trust.

——, 1977, *The Science of Self-Realisation,* Los Angeles, Bhaktivedanta Book Trust.

Richardson, James T., 1982, 'Conversion, brainwashing and deprogramming in new religions', *Update,* 6: 1, 34-49.

Robbins, Thomas, Anthony, Dick, and Richardson, James, 1978, 'Theory and research on today's new religions', *Sociological Analysis,* 39: 2, 95-122.

Robbins, Thomas, and Anthony, Dick, 1981, *In Gods We Trust: New Patterns of Religious Pluralism in America,* New Brunswick, Transaction Books.

Roszak, Theodore, 1970, *Making of a Counter-Culture,* London, Faber and Faber.

Singer, Milton (ed.), 1966, *Krishna: Myths, Rites and Attitudes,* Chicago, University of Chicago Press.

Wallis, Roy, 1984, *The Elementary Forms of the New Religious Life,* London, Routledge and Kegan Paul.

Werblowsky, R. J. Z., 1980, 'Religions new and not so new', *Numen,* 27: 1, 155-66.

Whitworth, John, and Shiels, Martin, 1982, 'From across the black water two imported varieties of Hinduism — the Hare Krishnas and the Ramakrishna Vedanta Society' in *New Religious Movements: A Perspective for Understanding Society,* ed. by Eileen Barker, New York, Edwin Mellen, 155-72.

Wilson, Bryan (ed.), 1981, *The Social Impact of New Religious Movements,* New York, Rose of Sharon Press.

Wuthnow, Robert, 1976, *The Consciousness Reformation,* Berkeley, University of California Press.

Zaehner, R. C., 1962, *Hinduism,* London, Oxford University Press.

Glossary

ADVAITA VEDANTA: the philosophical system attributed to **Shankara** characterized by a non-dualistic view of the Absolute in which the Supreme (**Brahman**) and the individual self (**Atman**) are one and the same.

ADVAITACARYA: a principal associate of **Chaitanya Mahaprabhu.**

ARATI: regular ritual in which a lighted lamp is rotated before temple deities.

ARJUNA: a warrior whose story is told in the *Bhagavad Gita* and to whom **Krishna** appears as counsellor, charioteer, friend, and Supreme Being.

ASHRAMA: the system of the four stages of life, See also **Brahmachari, Grihasta, Sannyasi.**

ATMAN: the self or soul. In **Krishna Consciousness** the spirit-soul is seen as related to but separate from the Supreme Soul. In **Advaita Vedanta** Atman is equated with **Brahman**, the Universal Absolute.

AVATARA: an incarnation; a manifestation of God on earth.

BACK TO GODHEAD: the monthly magazine of the Hare Krishna movement, produced in the United States but distributed internationally.

BENGALI: the language of much of the devotional literature of the Hare Krishna movement and its historical antecedent, the **Gaudiya Vaishnava Mission**.

BHAGAVAD GITA: the best-known and most widely-read of Indian scriptures, it records the conversation between Krishna and Arjuna at the battle of Kurukshetra.

BHAGAVAD GITA AS IT IS: Bhaktivedanta Swami Prabhupada's translation of the *Bhagavad Gita* with commentary. One of two important texts in the Hare Krishna movement. See also *Srimad Bhagavatam.*

BHAGAVANDAS GOSWAMI: the current spiritual leader for the UK. (His responsibilities also include Southern Europe, South Africa, Israel and Mauritius.)

BHAGAVATA PURANA: a devotional work from the Indian scriptural tradition which tells the story of Krishna, generally known in the Hare Krishna movement as *Srimad Bhagavatam.*

BHAKTA: a devotee of God. In Krishna Consciousness this designation is given to men in the preliminary stages of training, before initiation has been sought.

BHAKTI: devotion to God.

BHAKTI YOGA: the practice of devotion and devotional service.

BHAKTIN: a devotee of God. This term is used for women in the early stages of pre-initiation training.

BHAKTISIDDHANTA SARASWATI: the spiritual master of **Bhaktivedanta Swami** who gave the instruction that he should preach Krishna Consciousness in the West.

BHAKTIVEDANTA SWAMI: The founder of the International Society for Krishna Consciousness (**ISKCON**) and author of many books on the belief and practice of Krishna Consciousness; affectionately known as 'Prabhupada'.

BHAKTIVINODA THAKURA: the nineteenth-century founder of the **Gaudiya Vaishnava Mission**, and thus the 'great-grandfather' of **ISKCON**.

BRAHMACHARI: a male devotee in the first stage of life (**Ashrama**), dedicated to celibacy and study.

BRAHMACHARIN: a female devotee in the first stage of life (**Ashrama**), dedicated to celibacy and study.

BRAHMAN: the impersonal Absolute of the **Advaita Vedanta** philosophical system, but seen by theistic schools as the impersonal aspect of the Supreme Lord.

BRAHMIN: the highest of the four **Varnas**, the priestly class.

CHAITANYA MAHAPRABHU: the fifteenth-century saint who taught love of God through congregational chanting (**Sankirtana**), and who is seen as an **Avatara** of **Krishna** and the founder of the **Krishna Bhakti** practised by the Hare Krishna devotees.

DARSHAN: an opportunity to be in the presence of the **Deity** or the **Guru**; literally, to view or to see the deity.

DEITIES: temple statues which, once ceremonially installed, become the repositories of the divine characters they represent.

DEVOTEES: those who are committed to serving Krishna; members of the Hare Krishna movement.

DHARMA: social and religious law or duty.

DHOTI: lower garment made of cotton cloth worn with a long shirt (see **Kurta**) by men.

DVAITA: dualist philosophical system attributed to **Madhva** in which the souls and God are seen as entirely separate spiritual entities.

DVAITADVAITA: dualistic non-dualism in which at one and the same time God is both the same as and different from the individual souls; the system attributed to **Nimbarka**.

DWARKA: place in Gujarat in the West of India where Krishna spent his adult life as ruler.

FOLK: Friends of Lord Krishna; those members of the Hare Krishna movement who continue to live outside the temple communities and whose commitment to Krishna Consciousnes is combined with existing family and work ties.

FOLK MAGAZINE: the magazine which serves the FOLK membership in Britain.

GAUDIYA VAISHNAVA MISSION: the Bengali devotional movement founded in the nineteenth century which **Bhaktivedanta Swami** joined and in which the Hare Krishna movement has its roots.

GOPIS: the cowherd girl friends of Krishna; his most ardent devotees.

GOSWAMIS: the six Goswamis were followers of **Chaitanya Mahaprabhu** who, after his death, strove to propagate his preaching movement.

GRIHASTA: a person in the second of the four stages of life (**Ashrama**) in which devotees get married and become householders.

GURU: a spiritual master or teacher who takes disciples and leads them to self-realization.

GURUDEVA: the devotional name of the current spiritual master for the UK.

GURUPUJA: a ritual in which flowers are offered to the spiritual master.

HARINAMA: the holy name; the process of chanting the holy name.

ISKCON: International Society for Krishna Consciousness; the formal organization of the Hare Krishna movement, founded in 1966 in New York.

JANAMASHTAMI: the festival held to celebrate the anniversary of the birth of Krishna.

JAPA: chanting the names of God. In the Hare Krishna movement this is done using a string of wooden beads.

JIVA: the individual soul, which in the Chaitanya School is held to be the same as but separate from the Supreme Soul.

JNANA: knowledge.

KALI YUGA: the dark age in which we now live; the last of four ages of progressive degeneration.

KARMA: actions and their results in this and the next life.

KIRTANA: congregational chanting and dancing in glorification of God.

KRISHNA (Also KRSNA): one of the Hindu Gods but seen by most **Vaishnavas**, including Hare Krishna devotees, as the Supreme Being.

KRISHNA BHAKTI: the practice of devotion to Krishna.

KRISHNA CONSCIOUSNESS: the system by which a devotee becomes conscious of his or her true spiritual nature as a servant of Krishna.

KRSNADASA KAVIRAJA: the seventeenth-century devotee who compiled *Sri Caitanya-caritamrta*, the biography of **Chaitanya Mahaprabhu**.

KURTA: long shirt worn by men.

MADHVA: the thirteenth-century philosopher responsible for the dualistic school of thought (**Dvaita**); seen by Hare Krishna devotees as a teacher in the spiritual lineage of Krishna Consciousness.

MAHA MANTRA: the verse attributed by devotees with most potency in the current age; the Hare Krishna mantra: 'Hare Krishna, Hare Krishna, Krishna Krishna, Hare Hare, Hare Rama, Hare Rama, Rama Rama, Hare Hare'.

MAHABHARAT TIMES: the magazine produced by **ISKCON** to serve the Indian community in Britain.

MAHABHARATA: the Indian epic of which the *Bhagavad Gita* is a part.

MANDIR: Hindu temple.

MANGALARTI: the first religious service of the day in Hare Krishna temples.

MANTRA: a word or verse which possesses divine power.

MATHURA: the place where Krishna lived after leaving his childhood home in **Vrndavana**.

MAYA: the material illusory energy of God which deludes people into forgetfulness of their real, spiritual selves.

MOKSHA: liberation from the cycle of repeated birth and death.

MURTI: the name given to divine images once they have been ceremonially installed. See **Deities**.

NAMAJAPA: chanting the names of God.

NCHT: National Council of Hindu Temples.

NIMBARKA: the thirteenth-century religious leader responsible for the philosophical interpretation known as **Dvaitadvaita** or dualistic non-dualism.

NITYANANDA: the brother and close associate of **Chaitanya Mahaprabhu**.

PARAMPARA: Spiritual lineage; chain of disciplic succession.

PRABHUPADA: The founder of **ISKCON** and author of many books on the subject of Krishna Consciousness. Also known as **Bhaktivedanta Swami**.

PRABHUPADA-LILAMRTA: the six-volume biography of the founder of the Hare Krishna movement by Satsvarupa dasa Goswami.

PRASADAM: food which has been offered to Krishna and then shared amongst those present.

PUJA: worship; religious practices in which the deity is served.

PUJARI: ritual specialist, or priest, responsible for serving the temple deities.

RADHA: the intimate consort of Krishna; leader of the **Gopis** and resident of **Vrndavana**.

RAMA: an incarnation of God best known for his activities as King of Ayodhya, narrated in the *Ramayana*. Seen by many Hindus as an **Avatara** of **Vishnu** but by the majority of Krishna devotees, including those in **ISKCON**, as an incarnation of **Krishna**.

RAMANUJA: the twelfth-century religious leader associated with the philosophical system known as **Visishtadvaita** or qualified non-dualism which posed the first serious theistic threat to the monistic system of **Shankara**.

RAMAYANA: the Indian epic relating the story of **Rama**, his wife Sita, his brother Lakshman and the monkey leader Hanuman, and their victory over the demon Ravana.

RUKMINI: the wife of Krishna. After spending his childhood and youth in

Vrndavana Krishna went to **Mathura** and from there to **Dwarka** in West India. It was there that he met Rukmini and married her.

RUPA GOSWAMI: one of the six **Goswamis** who followed the teachings of **Chaitanya Mahaprabhu** and continued his mission after his death.

SADHU: a Hindu holy man.

SAMSARA: the cycle of repeated birth and death.

SANATANA DHARMA: eternal law or tradition; a term generally used by Hindus to refer to the antiquity of their religion and the duty of the individual within it.

SANATANA GOSWAMI: one of the six **Goswamis** who followed the teachings **Chaitanya Mahaprabhu** and continued his mission after his death.

SANKIRTANA: congregational chanting of the names of God, and, by extension, the whole preaching mission derived from the teachings of **Chaitanya Mahaprabhu**, the leader who first recommended this method of chanting as suitable for bringing souls to Krishna in this dark age.

SANNYASA: the rite of renunciation in which a person casts off all attachment to material objects and to friends and family.

SANNYASI: a person in the fourth stage of life: a renunciate or ascetic.

SANSKRIT: the language of **Vedic** literature still used in most of the rituals of the Hare Krishna movement.

SARI: a dress worn by female devotees.

SHANKARA: the ninth-century philosopher responsible for the system known as **Advaita Vedanta** or non-dualism in which a complete identity between the individual self and the Universal Absolute is taught.

SIKHA: the tail of hair worn by male devotees.

SRI CAITANYA-CARITAMRTA: the biography of **Chaitanya Mahaprabhu** written in the seventeenth century by **Krsnadasa Kaviraja** and translated into English by **Bhaktivedanta Swami**.

SRIMAD BHAGAVATAM: one of several religious texts valued by the Hare Krishna movement (see also *Bhagavad Gita* and *Sri Caitanya-caritamrta*). Otherwise known as the *Bhagavata Purana*, this work tells the story of Lord Krishna, and stresses the importance of devotion and service in his name.

SWAMI: a person who has become master of his senses; a spiritual master.

TILAKA: the off-white marks worn on the foreheads of devotees of the Hare Krishna movement signifying their allegiance to **Vaishnavism**.

UPANISHADS: those speculative, philosophical texts which form the latter part of the *Vedas*.

VAISHNAVA: one who serves **Vishnu**, **Krishna**, or **Rama**.

VAISHNAVA BHAKTI: devotion to **Vishnu**, **Krishna**, or **Rama**.

VAISHNAVISM: the form of worship and belief associated with the deities **Vishnu**, **Krishna**, or **Rama**.

VARNA: the Indian four-fold system of occupational classes in which the **Brahmin** or priestly class is the highest in terms of ritual status.

VEDANTA: the *Upanishads* and, by extension, their philosophy.

VEDANTA SUTRA: a compendium of Upanishadic teachings by Badarayana which has provided a focus for philosophical debate. See **Shankara, Ramanuja**, and **Madhva**.

VEDAS: the earliest Indian religious texts.

VEDIC: that which pertains to the culture and religion of the early texts.

VISHNU: a Hindu deity, worshipped by Krishna devotees as a manifestation of the Supreme Being, **Krishna**, but seen by other Hindus as the God from whom Krishna himself emanated.

VISISHTADVAITA: the philosophical system attributed to **Ramanuja**; qualified non-dualism.

VRNDAVANA: the birthplace of **Krishna**, associated with his pastimes with **Radha** and the **Gopis**.

Index